TWAYNE'S WORLD AUTHORS SERIES

A Survey of the World's Literature

SWEDEN

Leif Sjöberg, State University of New York at Stony Brook

EDITOR

Lars Gyllensten

TWAS 473

Lars Gyllensten

LARS GYLLENSTEN

By HANS ISAKSSON
University of Stockholm

Translated from the Swedish by
KATY LISSBRANT

TWAYNE PUBLISHERS
A DIVISION OF G. K. HALL & CO., BOSTON

Library of Congress Cataloging in Publication Data

Isaksson, Hans, 1942–
    Lars Gyllensten.

    (Twayne's world authors series ; TWAS 473)
    Bibliography: pp. 189–92
    1. Gyllensten, Lars Johan Wictor, 1921–
2. Authors, Swedish—20th century—Biography.
PT9875.G95Z74   1978   839.7′3′74   77–15551
ISBN 0–8057–6314–7

5-25-78

Contents

About the Author

Hans Isaksson was born in Sweden in 1942 and was educated at the University of Stockholm. He began by studying philosophy and then continued with literature. In the spring of 1974 he received his doctorate in literature with a dissertation on the narrative methods in Lars Gyllensten's novels. Dr. Isaksson has also written literary criticism for many years and is presently the editor of Bonnier's literary magazine (Stockholm), one of Sweden's foremost literary periodicals.

Preface

The Swedish novelist, Lars Gyllensten, made his début toward the end of the 1940's and by 1976 had published twenty books. His authorship soon awakened interest and has often been at the center of the Swedish literary debate. He is still active as an author.

From the very beginning, Sören Kierkegaard was Gyllensten's most important teacher. Gyllensten was especially fascinated by Kierkegaard's aesthetic method of exploring and contrasting different "stages" of life. He has, in fact, worked in a similar way throughout the whole of his own authorship: he has, in his novels, consciously and consistently formed and tested a series of different attitudes toward life. This method implies that his writings, to a greater extent than most other authors', comprise an integrated whole in which the single books both complement each other and argue against each other. Together, in an Existential spirit, they present us with a collection of examples of how we might adjust ourselves to existence.

But at the same time Gyllensten is very much an author who has moved with the times. The point of departure for his Existential exploration is the feeling that World War II ended in total political and moral bankruptcy. All of the main political ideologies and recognized philosophies seemed to him to be corrupt and the whole of his work can actually be seen as the expression of a passionate attempt at discovering a tenable and appropriate *modus vivendi*. In his earlier novels he developed a reserved and skeptical point of view which is reminiscent of the life style Albert Camus let Sisyphus incarnate in *The Myth of Sisyphus*. But toward the middle of the 1960's Gyllensten gradually moved away from this position and instead, under the influence of various metaphysical or mythical ideas, sought out a new and more positive attitude toward life.

It is this fascinating and radical development which I shall trace in my book. In the first chapter I shall describe the historical experiences which left their mark on Gyllensten and the epistemological ideas which decisively determined the formation of his writing. In the following chapters I shall deal with the different phases of his work, treating the novels in chronological order. In the final chapter I shall attempt to describe the new attitude Gyllensten arrived at. Thomas Mann is another of Gyllensten's teachers and like him, Gyllensten is both a clearly intellectual author as well as an author who is committed to profound psychological questions. In my interpretations of Gyllesten's novels I have attempted to do justice both to the philosophical discussions and to the emotional depths.

Technically I have attempted to make the presentation as simple as possible. All of the quotations from Gyllensten's books are translated by Katy Lissbrant. The notes are primarily for those readers who wish to continue with Gyllensten's writings on their own. The page references after the quotations from Gyllensten's books refer to the original publications in Swedish. As regards *Cain's Memoirs*, however, page references are also given to Keith Bradfield's English translation from 1967 entitled *The Testament of Cain*.

HANS ISAKSSON

The University of Stockholm

Chronology

1890   Carl Gyllensten, Lars Gyllensten's father, born in Björne-
        borg, Finland.
1894   Ingrid Rangström, his mother, born in Stockholm. Sister
        of the Swedish composer Ture Rangström.
1920   Carl Gyllensten marries Ingrid Rangström.
1921   Lars Johan Wictor Gyllensten born in Stockholm on
        November 12.
1923 and 1924: His sisters Ulla and Britta born.
1922–24, 1928–32, and 1936–45: The family spends long sum-
        mers in the Stockholm archipelago. Impressions from
        these summers appear in his books.
1925–27 and 1933–35: Similar long summers on a farm in south-
        ern Sweden near the small town of Eksjö. Memories from
        this locale and the town also appear in his writings.
1927   His youngest sister Ingalill born. Danger to his mother's
        life. Death of his grandfather. Feelings of insecurity—
        strong fear of the possibility that his mother might carry
        yet another child and risk the same danger.
1932   His father goes bankrupt. Economic crisis in the family,
        but the father manages to regain a stable economy.
1937–   Increasing reading of philosophy, among others Kant,
1939   Schopenhauer, Nietzsche and modern epistemology, in-
        cluding theories of natural science. Begins more systematic
        studies of philosophy. 1938–39: growing thoughts of
        becoming an author—starts making notes.
1939   First acquaintance with the writings of Sören Kierkegaard.
1940   Matriculation in Stockholm. Begins his studies at the Caro-
        line Institute (the medical university of Stockholm).
1946   Married to Inga-Lisa Hultén, fellow student at the med-
        ical university. The hoax—a mock book of "modern"
        poetry, *Camera obscura*, published anonymously (pen-
        name Jan Wictor) co-authored with his friend Torgny
        Greitz. Great alarm in the press.

1948 Medicine Licenciat, and registered physician. Continues scientific work at the Caroline Institute—department of histology.

1949 First serious book, *Modern Myths*, published.

1950 *The Blue Ship* published. Starts contributing to the Liberal newspaper *Dagens Nyheter* (Stockholm). His reviews and debate articles often initiate prolonged and heated public discussions and make him a controversial person, attacked from many quarters.

1952 Publishes *Infantilia*.

1953 His daughter Katarina born. Doctor of medicine on an experimental thesis about the regulation of the growth of lymph nodes and other lymphatic organs. Assistant Professor (*Docent*) at the Caroline Institute, Stockholm. *Carnivora* published.

1955 Associate Professor (*Prosektor*) at the Caroline Institute. Research on oxygen-induced eye disease in new born children and on functional influences on the development of the visual system. Studies of blood cell production. Publishes articles warning against German nationalism.

1956 *Senilia* published.

1957– Involved in intense public debate concerning nuclear
1960 bomb tests and atomic weapons, warns against Swedish armament with nuclear bombs.

1958 Publishes *The Senator*. 1958–72: On several different occasions publishes criticism of medical experiments with patients and articles on medical ethics.

1960 His father dies. *The Death of Socrates* published.

1962 *Desperadoes* published.

1963 *Cain's Memoirs* published.

1964 *Nihilistic Credo* published.

1965 *Juvenilia* published. Warns against German neo-Nazism, argues for a Swedish recognition of East Germany and of the present borders in Germany and Europe. He is attacked for these articles.

1966 He is elected member of the Swedish Academy and, from 1968 on, member of the Nobel Committee for literature. *Lotus in Hades* published.

Chronology

1967–   Member of the board of the Swedish Broadcasting Com-
1974   pany. Involved in several debates concerning mass com-
        munication, the changing roles of journalists and bureau-
        cratism of cultural communication.

1968   Publishes *Diarium Spirituale*. Articles against anti-human
        city planning and dangers of modern urbanization.

1970   *The Palace in the Park* published.

1971   *From My Public Sector* and *Man, Animals, All of Nature*
        published.

1973   Left the Caroline Institute. *The Cave in the Desert* pub-
        lished.

1975   *In the Shadow of Don Juan* published. He is elected
        member of the Royal Swedish Academy of Sciences.

1976   *Patchwork Quilts – Tokens of Life* (excerpts from his
        note books) published. He criticizes sharply the Palme
        administration for its nuclear energy policy and argues
        for voting against it in the parliamentary elections, after
        having supported the Social Democrats previously.

1977   He is appointed Permanent Secretary of the Swedish
        Academy.

CHAPTER 1

The Bankruptcy of Naïveté

I Biographical Sketch

L ARS Gyllensten was born in Stockholm in 1921, and has lived there ever since.[1] His family may be described as middle-class. His father, Carl Gyllensten, grew up under relatively meager circumstances, but managed to acquire a business education for himself both at home and abroad. He became director of the Swedish branch of a German machinery firm, dealt in other business affairs, and amassed considerable wealth during the twenties. He lost everything in the great economic crash of 1932, in connection with the death of the Swedish financial magnate Ivar Kreuger, but was later able to build up a new fortune. The family's shifting economic conditions led to several moves between different apartments in Stockholm, all, however, in well-to-do districts. The Östermalm area is an especially recurrent locale in Gyllensten's novels.

In spite of the moves, the life of the family was for the most part free from dramatic events. Lars was the first-born and he later had three sisters. However, in 1927, when his mother Ingrid (née Rangström), was to have her last child, complications arose. His mother had a nearly fatal hemorrhage during the delivery and there was also a risk that the child would die. The five-to-six-year-old Lars surmised the seriousness of the situation and for the remainder of his childhood was plagued by the fear that his mother would once again have to go to the "baby-house." He faced this fear with the help of different kinds of magic rituals all of which were meant to safeguard the number four. For example he divided objects into groups of four and recited four evening prayers at a time in four different positions in bed. A fifth child must simply not be allowed to come into the world. That same year another episode took

13

place which was less far-reaching but which nonetheless remained in his thoughts. At Christmas while Lars and his
maternal grandfather were walking hand in hand to the dinner
table, Lars pulled eagerly; and his grandfather fell and sprained
his hand. Later in the spring his grandfather contracted cancer
and died. For the five–six-year-old it seemed for awhile as if
he were partly responsible for his grandfather's death.

A certain amount of tension existed between his parents which
was due partly to their different temperaments and partly to
the existing pattern of family roles. The father's business activities were pressing at times; and he could be irascible, impatient,
and choleric. On the other hand, his mother, who had stayed
at home as a housewife after her marriage, was sensitive
and fragile. When conflicts arose, the children became frightened
and took their mother's part. The result was a disturbance in
their contact with their father, causing timidity and even fear.
In time feelings of guilt arose because they were not able to
respond to their father's attempts at showing affection. It was
only later that they understood that they had perhaps been
too easily upset by the temper of their father. There is surely
a relationship between these experiences and the isolated, older
fathers who appear in several of Gyllensten's novels.

Gyllensten chose primarily scientific subjects in high school
but was at the same time interested in literature and philosophy.
In puberty he became deeply involved in Existential questions.
He intensely experienced the "onceness" of his own life and
the importance of living it in a meaningful way. Of all that
one could do in the world, much was in his eyes nothing more
than mania and diversion. Thus he found it even more
important to discover that which was truly urgent and meaningful—a theme which is also sustained throughout his literary
production. His literary and philosophical interests were reinforced, and he also began to formulate his thoughts in aphoristic
notes.

These Existential questions were especially expressed in his
choice of a profession, which he felt to be very decisive. During
his high school years it had seemed obvious that he would continue with some type of scientific education, but face to face
with the necessity of making the choice himself, he became

doubtful and filled with anxiety. The summer after graduation he was torn between different alternatives; he studied Latin, among other things, in order eventually to be able to study philosophy and the history of literature at the University of Stockholm. To him all professions, in themselves, seemed to be limiting and mutilating. Choice felt more like rejection and entering one of many narrow cages. At the last minute he sent in applications to both the Technical University and the Caroline Institute (the medical university of Stockholm)—still keeping the possibility of studying philosophy open. The reason that he finally chose medicine was the broad spectrum of the subject from physics and biology to sociology and psychology. Medicine was the least restrictive choice.

Gyllensten began at the Caroline Institute in the autumn of 1940 but found the studies mechanical and without personal relevance. He studied half-heartedly for a few years and during certain periods asked himself almost daily whether or not he should stop.[2] He continued with his philosophical reading at the same time and also continued to work on the elucidation of his positions in diary form. Eventually, though, he came in touch with medical research which sparked his interest. He began by chance in histology and continued his research in this area. He defended his doctor's dissertation in 1953 and two years later began working as associate professor at the Caroline Institute. Gyllensten himself has characterized his research as careful and useful, and in several areas his results drew international attention. He has, however, declared several times that he regards his literary authorship as more significant than his research.[3] In 1973 he resigned his position at the Caroline Institute in order to devote the remainder of his productive years to writing. In the long run writing showed itself to be the most important and challenging task he had discovered.

II *Historical Experiences*

In an autobiographical essay from 1956—"Lyckans värn mot våldet" ("The Defense of Happiness against Violence")—Gyllensten attempted to round up the historical experiences which were decisive in forming his way of looking at the world:

The Spanish Civil War signified a kind of first communion for many of the somewhat older friends in my generation. It was like a cold shower on youthful utopias. It twisted the dreams and wishes for a happier and more just future society, which was hopefully on its way, into bitter disappointment. It became a cynical and unmistakable exposition of the strong powers of brutality, chance, vulgarity, and cruelty in historical events. I was probably too young: the Spanish war passed me by, but in return Nazism in Germany had a corresponding significance.

To be sure, Gyllensten continued, Nazism revealed nothing totally new to him. He seemed to have discovered even earlier that "history is without morals or mercy" and that "people are equipped with all the resources to do all conceivable and more than conceivable, indescribable and unlimited evil deeds to their equals and fellow men." But the "mass crimes" of Nazism confirmed the case: "Nazism was the confirmation which revealed the face of the world naked and exposed behind the thin, cracked skin of propriety and forbearance." Nor did the end of the war lead to any clear and easily defined turn for the better:

Nazism was defeated, and pessimism could dally in more optimistic times—but in the last, triumphant stage of the war the winning powers, the representatives of the good, laid a couple of very special eggs like the well-known bird, the Roc. The atomic bombs dropped on Japan surpassed the military atrocities of the Germans during the whole war—death, suffering, and terror to hundreds of thousands of innocent people: women, children and the unborn, and to the children of the unborn and their children. This was not brought about by Nazi or Fascist states, but by the defenders of democracy and human rights. . . . This was the most atrocious victory that the representatives of the good could win in this atrocious war.[4]

I have quoted so extensively because the mode of expression bears witness to Gyllensten's violent reaction to Nazism and World War II. He seems to have reacted with fury and bitterness in a way which bordered on despair and complete pessimism, but also with a strong desire for clarity and a definite rejection of every attempt at seeing the events in a conciliatory light. In an article from 1949 he stated laconically that "There is no possibility or reason to excuse the war."[5] The war obviously was too atrocious for him to allow justification in any way. Furthermore, Gyllensten felt strongly that neither of the battling sides returned from the war guiltless. In another autobiographical essay—"Gryning mot väster" ("Dawn in the West")—Gyllensten wrote that he had already come in contact with Nazism in the middle of the 1930's. His father traveled extensively in Germany in his profession and returned home full of revulsion and scorn for the manifestations of Nazism. Later Gyllensten himself met the expressions of Nazism in Sweden—among other things he was once taken to a backyard by some older boys where, dressed in boots, they took part in exercises before an officious leader. These experiences led him to turn away from Germany at the end of the decade and to orient himself toward the West and the critical and empirical tradition which England represented.[6] But with the atomic bombs on Nagasaki and Hiroshima at the final stage of the war, "the representatives of the good" committed just as terrible a terrorist deed as the Nazis had practiced earlier thus making the allied victory equivocal. It was obviously impossible completely to declare one's solidarity with any of the warring sides. It is surely correct to regard the atomic bombs on Japan as a strong contributory cause for Gyllensten's refusal to reconcile himself with the war. Later, toward the end of the fifties, he would come to attack violently the Swedish military men who demanded that Sweden acquire her own atomic weapons.

I think it is important to underline that Nazism and World War II really left deep scars on Gyllensten. In Erik Hjalmar Linder's pertinent comment he was "burned by the Nazi epoch."[7] One can find further support for this view in the fact that Gyllensten returned to Nazism time after time in articles and essays. There is a German theme which can be followed throughout his works, and the fervor found in "The Defense of Happiness against Violence" recurs often in his later statements. He had already taken up Nazism in a few satirical pieces in his early prose book *Carnivora* from 1953, and in one of these he even mentioned the atomic bombs on Japan. In partly fragmented language he wrote, regarding some tourists who were taking pictures of the ruins of the castle in Heidelberg, "In Hiroshima there was very little left, Nagasaki hardly registers on the film" (129). An article in the Stockholm daily, *Dagens Nyheter,* (1965) stirred a great deal of attention when Gyllensten recommended Swedish diplomatic recognition of East Germany as a political means of combating the growing retaliatory and neo-Nazi currents in West Germany.[8] As late as 1972 he referred to the Nazi Olympics in 1936 in a newspaper article in order to throw light on the Nixon regime's tactics of terror bombing Indo-China behind the shield of spectacular space projects.[9] His experiences of Nazism have clearly remained vivid and significant for him—not the least in the understanding of current political events.

The feeling that none of the warring sides left World War II free of some share of guilt led Gyllensten to strong skepticism toward easygoing, optimistic hopes for a better future; and he also kept a critical distance from established political ideologies. Against all totalitarian pretentions, he wished instead to rely on democracy as a method for creating a better society step by step. Gyllensten developed these thoughts most extensively in an article written in 1959. There he maintained that the ideas and ideals we embrace today are "the swills and crumbs and drops from old relationships which we have already worn out." During the 1700's and 1800's the liberal ideas were full of promises for the future. Later the socialistic ideals also seemed "so bold and full of liberation and light." But today the situation is different: "now we no longer have any masters." We broke with liberalism when we saw that "the freedom of the strong was not the freedom of the weak." In the same way we are at cross purposes with "radical socialism" because of the experiences from the socialistic states which have emerged —he especially pointed out the leaders' misuse of power. Gyllensten above all rejected the totalitarian states of the 1900's, which primarily included Nazi Germany and Stalin's Soviet Union.[10]

The position which Gyllensten finally arrived at may be summarized in the following way: the great political ideologies—even the more refined ones such as liberalism and socialism—do not qualify as all-encompassing goals or as programs of action. Nor is it possible to arrive at a complete and irreproachable interpretation of reality with their help. Here is a later and very representative statement from Gyllensten:

Faced with critical investigation and reflection on the complex conditions of reality, the pretentious systems of dogma lose their authority and behave like fantasies or hypotheses, fascinating perhaps, beautifully constructed and stimulating for the imagination and will, but nonetheless time-bound works of men, marked by arbitrariness and simplification.[11]

This criticism did not mean, however, that Gyllensten completely rejected the great political ideologies. He seems to have felt that some of the ideas of liberalism and socialism were both just and sound. He described his own position in an interview (1967) by characterizing himself as "a conglomerate of ideas from socialism, liberalism, science, etc.—a bad thing for a true ideologue."[12] He apparently seems to have found the great political dogmas useful, in a limited way, as instruments for interpreting and understanding reality. Gyllensten's criticism of the political ideologies to a great extent ought to be regarded as an expression of his general skepticism of all such dogmas and theories which claim to hold absolute, authoritative, and definite knowledge.

III *Reflections on the Theory of Knowledge*

Gyllensten's earliest studies were oriented toward Germany. German was the first foreign language his generation learned in school and Germany was still the cultural country above all others. As far as fiction is concerned, he read mostly Goethe, Hoffman and Heine.[13] But at an early age he also plunged into a surprisingly comprehensive study of philosophy. He found an epistemological theme in Kant's teaching that our knowledge is determined by our forms of perception and categories of thought which captivated his interest from the very beginning. The idea that our way of seeing the world is formed by our resources for understanding reality is the *leitmotif* of his continued philosophical study, and he returns to it time and again in articles and essays. For him it has clearly been such an important insight that he continually worked at formulating and developing it in more precise and, as the years went by,

newer terms. It is therefore difficult to overestimate the significance of these epistemological ideas for his thinking and his
whole attitude toward life. In addition they definitely decided
the direction of his literary program. Gyllensten's attempts at
formulating his own epistemological position certainly are also
due to the fact that he regards it as important for the understanding of his writing.

In "Dawn in the West," Gyllensten stated that it was his early
interest in mathematics which led him to Kant:

It was mathematics which made Kant a Kantian and mathematics
made me in a way a Kantian. They pointed me in the direction of
a conviction that we human beings are in an important way enclosed
in our own human means and methods, secure but also imprisoned
in our own senses and our own words.[14]

According to Hans-Erik Johannesson, who traced Gyllensten's
philosophical studies in his doctoral dissertation, Gyllensten had
begun to read Kant as early as the summer of 1937. During the
next few years he discovered similar thoughts first in Schopenhauer and later in Kierkegaard. Schopenhauer impressed him
with his thesis of "the world as will and idea" and Kierkegaard
with the thought that truth is subjective. When Gyllensten began
to orient himself toward the West at the end of the 1930's, he
seems to have found the truth of the basic insight he had found
in Kant verified by the representatives of logical empiricism.
Through studies of Russell, Kaila, and von Wright, especially,
he came to attribute a growing importance to language in the
formation of our view of the world.[15] The two American episte-
mologists, Charles Sander Peirce and Percy Williams Bridgman,
had, however, greater significance for him than any of the
individual representatives of logical empiricism. In Bridgman's
The Logic of Modern Physics, Gyllensten could read that
scientific concepts are constructions which do not directly
correspond to characteristics of reality and that the results the
scientist arrives at are dependent upon the operations he must
perform in order to investigate reality at all. At this point
Gyllensten had personal experience in scientific research to
rely upon and was thus stimulated to go further in his scientific

studies. During the latter years he has primarily referred to the pragmatism of Peirce in determining his own epistemological position. Gyllensten seems to have been especially fascinated by Peirce's presentation of scientific work as a continuous, constantly revised, and never-ending investigation of reality, an "infinite inquiry."

Gyllensten presented a representative and clear formulation of the epistemological position he had arrived at in an article in 1965 in which he rejected all forms of naive realism:

Our understanding of reality is dependent upon our linguistic means of interpreting reality. There is a mutual influence between reality and language—the resources of language determine our understanding and experiencing of reality, and our experiences of reality in turn form our language and stimulate us to enrich it; there is what neuro-physiologists and others call a "feedback" relationship between reality and language. There is therefore no "normal," "ordinary," or obvious simple understanding of what is real.[16]

According to Gyllensten, his view of, broadly speaking, our linguistic means, even includes scientific research. The language which science uses consists of theories and models and they to a certain degree determine the results of the research. Furthermore, it is not necessarily true that one theory alone is the only conceivable and useful one for understanding the reality investigated. On the contrary, most of the sciences use contradictory theories. Thus a subjective or conventional element is involved even in the strictest scientific research: the research reflects the researcher's experiences and scientific schooling. Also, it ought to be emphasized that Gyllensten sees scientific activity as a dialectic process. With his theory the researcher understands the facts in which he is interested, but at the same time new facts force him to develop his theory. Knowledge arises in the continuous interaction between theory and fact.

But Gyllensten also regards ideologies and philosophies of life as languages which interpret reality for the people who believe in them. Even the individual's language—often composed of elements from different ideologies and with individual characteristics—to a significant degree determines how he experiences reality. To underline the intimate interdependence between language and reality he has compared language to one of the organs of the senses: language forms the world we experience all around us just as much as our eyes do. In one of the many articles in which he developed these ideas, Gyllensten wrote that for the person who possesses a religious language, the world is perhaps a "bridge between good and evil, a place where the devil and God have a meeting place." On the other hand, the person who is politically oriented perhaps thinks that he is living in "a game, where there is no other right than that of the strongest, and no other value than that lying in the victory of one's own group." And furthermore:

No one can claim that all of these different worlds are the same, that in the end they are all alike. Only he who is so firmly anchored in his own view that he is not able to perceive anything else can say that they are mere products of imagination.[17]

Gyllensten also regards this more general relationship between language and reality as dialectic. The language we are in command of determines how we experience reality, but at the same time new experiences help our language to develop further and thus even our view of reality is altered. In an analysis of the linguistic work in which he is involved as an author, Gyllensten described these dialectics in a very characteristic way:

Language is an organ of the senses. There our forms and norms meet the realm of the extraordinary and coincidental and tame it with their categories, describe it and experience it as fully as our resources permit. But language, in this broad meaning, can also be changed, it can alter itself and let itself be altered by that which it meets.[18]

Gyllensten's epistemological view implies that scientific knowledge can never be absolutely sure and definite. Nor can one philosophy of life rule alone or be taken as the given point of departure. Thus the naive faith that the knowledge of the world which we possess today is completely authoritative is undermined. On the contrary, all knowledge is incomplete and provisory. We live, one could say, right in the midst of a continuous process of knowledge. This complex of ideas is not only a main theme in Gyllensten's essays, it is also an experience he constantly returns to in his novels, and in several of them he has directly described different ways of meeting it. In this way all of his novels together express a complex reaction. On the one hand these epistemological conditions mean that there is no truth which is completely independent of human beings. Our knowledge is our own picture of how the world is created and, using a Kantian turn, it can be said that we can never reach reality in itself. Here there is a limit to our ability and power. Perhaps we may even experience our means of understanding as a prison out of which we cannot escape. But on the other hand this situation means that we constantly receive new knowledge and possibilities. In this way Gyllensten's epistemological view is also a challenge to continual and exciting development. We are not thrown into an unchanging world but instead have the possibility of creating our own reality to a great extent.

IV *The Generation of the 1940's*

In the epilogue of his first book, *Moderna myter* (*Modern Myths*), Gyllensten attempted to summarize both his experiences of World War II and his epistemological views with an expressive phrase: "the bankruptcy of naïveté." It ought to be emphasized that there is a strong and profound agreement between his historical experiences and his theoretical views. It is also reasonable to assume that Gyllensten's view of contemporary historical events and his epistemological views developed through a process of mutual influence. The growth of Nazi ideology with its primitive myths seems especially to have led him to the view that our knowledge in many respects is based on a fragile human foundation. At the same time the fact that all of the great political ideologies seemed to have been compromised by World War II confirmed the correctness of his epistemological view. The unity between historical experiences and theoretical views primarily lay in the fact that it was a question of retreat

and defeat in both cases: the feeling that the great political
ideologies had collapsed corresponded on the theoretical level
with a collapse in the hope of being able to arrive at completely true and definite knowledge. It was a question of a
strong feeling of bankruptcy on both the historical and the
theoretical levels.

It was especially in this emotional atmosphere that Gyllensten's writing shared common ground with the reactions and
positions of that generation of Swedish authors which emerged
during the 1940's. The similarities are, for example, striking
between Gyllensten's early positions and the viewpoints of the
influential poet and critic, Karl Vennberg (b. 1910) during the
1940's. Gyllensten's own comments about his writing indicate
that he felt affinity with the writers of the 1940's. In several of
his essays, the generation of the 1940's is the obvious point of
departure when he formulates his own esthetic goals, and in
an article in 1953 he declared that he felt more at home in the
1940's than in the 1950's.[19] In general there is a clearly delineated
participation and solidarity in everything he wrote about the
experiences and struggles of the generation of the 1940's. But
at the same time Gyllensten was considerably younger than
the leading authors of the 1940's and did not make his debut
until 1949. It is therefore probable that he not only shared
important experiences with the older writers of the 1940's, but
was also stimulated by them during the years in which he
oriented himself toward his own authorship. For example, before
his own debut Vennberg published the two significant collections
of poetry *Halmfackla* (1944) and *Tideräkning* (1945); and in
a later commentary Gyllensten declared that he, with his early
writing and criticism, in some respects had been his teacher.[20]
Perhaps Vennberg became so significant because he gave a
literary form to the same ideas that Gyllensten himself had
arrived at through his philosophical studies and thus helped
to encourage Gyllensten on the way to fiction. In other words,
Gyllensten shared the basic experiences of the writers of the
1940's and was also able to follow paths related to those that
they had staked out.

The points of contact between Gyllensten and the other
writers of the 1940's are fairly clear. The generation of the

1940's consisted of many very different writers, but it is still obvious that World War II was an overshadowing experience for most of them. It also seems as if Sweden's special position in the historical events formed their experiences significantly. Sweden was outside of the war and they were thus able to follow it as spectators. For several years they felt the war coming like something unavoidable, and during the terrible war years they saw large areas of Europe become ruins. The catastrophe took place before their eyes without their being able to influence it; and they reacted with resignation, despair, and perhaps even feelings of guilt because they were spared. But at the same time Sweden's neutral position provided them with greater possibilities for critical distance than those who had the war upon them. In any case, the experiences of the war led them to profound skepticism, which they expressed during the years after the war. Erik Hjalmar Linder has pointed out this skeptical attitude to all ideological systems as one of the important common denominators for the writers of the 1940's. He has sought the reasons for this skepticism primarily in the confusing series of events, seen ideologically, which led to World War II: Hitler's growing threat to Europe, Chamberlain's concessions in Munich, the Spanish Civil War like a public dress rehearsal of the coming war, and finally the almost incredible pact between Nazi Germany and the Soviet Union. But he also points out that the skepticism of the writers of the 1940's must be seen against the background of the period between the wars with its many currents of ideas each with great pretensions—in Sweden primitivism, psychoanalysis and sometimes even socialism were especially elevated to dogmas of salvation.[21] The older writers of the 1940's seem to have experienced the 1930's as a time of feverish ideological formulations, to which the war later put a terrible stop.

One of Vennberg's often quoted lines from an article on modern pessimism reveals how complete this experience could be: "Behind us lie, unsolved or only half-way settled, all the great crises in ideas: the crisis of socialism, of Christianity, of humanism, of psychology, and of politics."[22] In Vennberg at least, this skepticism toward all established ideologies could also glide into a skepticism about the possibilities of ever reaching the

truth. In the introductory poem in *Halmfackla* he wrote, with
a turn of phrase typical for Vennberg's writing from the 1940's:

> The face
> which is stamped on real coins
> is the same which false coins reveal.[23]

The other great poet of the generation of the 1940's was
Erik Lindegren (1910–68), and the title of his most influential
collection of poems was no less revealing: *mannen utan väg*
(1942; Eng. tr. in *New Directions 21*, 1969, as *the man without
a way*). Did any road exist at all away from the murder, torture,
and lies of the war, he seemed to ask. Similar emotional tones
were also heard from the novelists. In *Ormen* (*The Snake*),
Stig Dagerman (1923–54) described how the horrors of the
times oozed out of the cracks in the floors even in the Swedish
military bases, and Sivar Arnér (b. 1909) took an extreme
pacifist position in his first book. As Gunnar Brandell has underlined, it is characteristic that the writers of the 1940's were
very critical toward the morale building literature produced by
many older writers toward the end of the 1930's and the
beginning of the 1940's.[24] Personally they did not feel they could
see any nation or political system which they could support
whole-heartedly.

Also common for several of the writers of the 1940's was the
fact that they did not formulate their criticism of the official
ideologies from any existing or new ideology, but rather from
a demand for awareness and analysis. The skepticism toward
the political systems which they felt they had seen compromised
during the war, seems to have given them the need to keep
a distance from all ideologies and systems of dogma in general.
Thus, for example, Vennberg asked whether "analysis, which
reveals the blindness of us all and which, beyond all systems
of thought, refers the central question back to the human being
and the nature of the human being, was not actually the appropriate action."[25] This same principle is expressed on a more
theoretical level in Gyllensten's epistemological views. When
he emphasizes the subjective element in all knowledge and
maintains the necessity of the continuous testing of knowledge,

he too is pleading for concentration on awareness and analysis. It was also from Vennberg that Gyllensten took up the term "faithless" in some parts of his work to characterize the critical and open position he aimed at.

However, it is important to see the skepticism of the writers of the 1940's against the background of the fact that they felt themselves to be living through a profoundly serious crisis. For them the war seemed to be a hopeless catastrophe and there were no new possibilities for life in sight. Their skepticism was far from any kind of supercilious attitude; instead it had its roots in despair and an extreme pessimism. At the same time, however, their will to awareness and criticism meant a form of resistance which counteracted total pessimism. As Erik Hjalmar Linder has pointed out, the compactness of their position bears a striking resemblance to that form of Existentialism which was presented by Sartre and Camus during World War II—both were translated into Swedish in 1946 and drew a great deal of attention. In spite of the fact that they represented an almost total pessimism, they paradoxically spoke of the decisive significance of action.[26] But the comparison ought not to be taken too far. In retrospect Gyllensten described the emotional atmosphere the Swedish writers of the 1940's experienced in the following way:

An extremely complex and challenging feeling of catastrophe and defeat gave resonance, but was balanced by other kinds of involvement—defiance, protest, revolt, and sympathy in a battle for life, the bastions of which seemed to lie primarily in the individual and in the pathetic decisions of private persons or small groups of fellow-believers united in a front against the established societies and institutions of power.[27]

It is important to understand that it was in this atmosphere of catastrophe and defeat that Gyllensten laid the foundation of his authorship. In many respects what he calls "the bankruptcy of naïveté" is also a crisis with all that it involves of ideological collapse and disappointed ideals. The epilogue of *Modern Myths* is written in a bantering tone which is directed against a too pathetic seriousness, but one can still feel the breadth and depth of the crisis in a few expressive formulations. In an introductory definition of this position, Gyllensten expresses the situation in the following way: "dropped off behind the wagon, with nothing to hold on to." And the solution to this situation is "to hold oneself by the hand and wander on" (168). This last phrase captures not only the general intellectual means by which Gyllensten wanted to meet "the bankruptcy of naïveté," but also indicates the direction of his literary ambitions as they were represented in this first book of his series of "existential explorations."

V *Literary Program*

Gyllensten has had a very strong theoretical interest in his own work as an author ever since he began writing. He made a first major attempt at declaring his aesthetic positions as early as 1950, when his second book was published. Since then he has discussed aesthetic questions time and again in essays and articles and has sought to clarify his own literary program. But he has also taken up the aesthetic problems which engaged him in other contexts: in the forewords and epilogues he has included in his books, in independent commentaries on his books, in reviews and polemical articles and, not least, in the novels themselves. All of these expositions bear witness to his persistent efforts to clarify and communicate the aesthetic goals which lay behind his books. Thus, his struggle with aesthetic questions must be seen as an important part of his authorship.

Gyllensten came in contact with the epistemological ideas which engaged him throughout his work while still in his youth. In the same way, he seems to have adhered early in his career to certain aesthetic ideas which were decisive for him—there is, in fact, a very important connection between his epistemological views and the aesthetic position he takes which I shall return to. Later, he continued to explore these aesthetic ideas, and as his reading became more extensive he attempted to use some new terms to make them more precise. But the aesthetic positions in his articles from the 1960's and the beginning of the 1970's are still basically the same that he had already adopted in his earliest articles. He has used different techniques and forms in different phases of his authorship—in this respect there is a continuous development in his books. But in my opinion, the basic aesthetic program remains the same throughout the whole of his writing. Perhaps it is not only to make his aesthetic goals more precise that Gyllensten has written about them repeatedly. It also seems as though from time to time he had a need to return to his original positions to rediscover the central line of his writing and then to advance in new directions. It seems probable that the aesthetic ideas have strongly stimulated his creativity.

In some of his earliest essays Gyllensten began by firmly rejecting two, in his opinion, untenable literary tendencies so that he could then formulate his own program more clearly. One of these two tendencies is realism. In his very first "program article"—"Ord: Notiser till ett författarskap" ("Words: Comments on an Authorship")—he frankly declared, "A common misunderstanding is that writing should be descriptive, should relate a reality existing somewhere and sometime."[28] One of Gyllensten's objections to realism has to do with the fact that there is no longer any common and general reality left to describe after the upheavals of World War II—in another of his early articles he spoke, referring primarily to Nazism, of "the lost reality."[29] Here he not only referred specifically to Europe's ruined cities, but also to the many ideologies and norms which the war had invalidated. But behind Gyllensten's rejection of realism also lay a theoretical criticism which seems to have been more decisive. In "Words: Comments on an Authorship," he rejected the ambition of Lars Ahlin, the Swedish novelist (b. 1915), to identify himself with the people he wrote about. In the beginning of the 1940's Ahlin emerged as a very independent novelist and his thinking on aesthetic questions probably influenced Gyllensten in the direction of the position he came to take. But Gyllensten rejected the idea of identification:

How can one identify with anyone else? As if anyone else had existed before one "identified"! Can anyone be saved without first creating him, his sin, his need, his mercy? How does one know that one hasn't identified the other with oneself instead of oneself with the other . . .[30]

The foundation of these almost paradoxical formulations lies in Gyllensten's epistemological views. In his way of thinking, identifying oneself with another person always involves a measure of subjective interpretation—it is in this respect that one "creates," to a certain degree, the person one identifies with. Thus an author who wishes to describe another person through identification is in reality giving his own picture of the nature of this person. What he really is doing is less a question of identification than of incarnation: he goes into the person he is describing. In more general terms this means that each description of reality is colored by the author's experiences, education, and linguistic means. Therefore even the most objective description of reality is in the end an interpretation of reality.

In opposition to the ambition of the realists to render reality, Gyllensten has instead emphasized that writing is a creation of man and a product of art: an artifact. In another program article from the middle of the 1950's he claimed that all literature in some way or other is surrealistic and continued,

It joins together a unique and self-willed pattern of fragments taken from reality. These fragments can be fairly concrete and realistic, and perhaps ought to be so to make a better impression. But a creation emerges in the new pattern which has nothing to do with ordinary reality. Just as a church or a house is built of stones and mortar and other things from nature which nevertheless become something unnatural and created by man, so is literature something self-willed and constructed, even the most psychological and humanly descriptive novel which seems packed with realities out of nature. It actually says nothing about reality—it is a new reality.[31]

In other words, the writer uses material from reality, but at the same time forms this material into an artificial creation. The quotation's last sentence is, however, polemically sharp. The statement that writing is a new reality is directed against the belief that written works as a whole paint a picture of reality. But the statement that writing says nothing about reality does not mean that it is not related to reality. In an article a few years later, Gyllensten once again asserted that the written work does not describe "anything which exists" and in the following way made the relation between fiction and reality more precise:

> On the other hand, the work of an author means t'   one creates a relationship to reality. With the help of language, the author puts himself in a relationship with the world around him. He gathers material from all areas, which he thinks he can use for his work in some way, and later he forms this material in a fashion which means that he establishes himself in relation to it and wants to do something with it.[32]

One can say that Gyllensten specifically turned against all ten dencies to confuse literature and reality. Writing is a matter of taking up one's position in relation to reality, and it is just as well to own up to the fact openly—thus can his criticism of realism be summarized.

The other literary goal which Gyllensten rejects is auto biographical writing. When he began writing he declared,

> The personal, as a manifestation alone, is unimportant in an ob jective context. The surge of anxiety, puberty's misgivings, the soldier's discomfort in the barracks or the indignation of an authoress at not being accepted by the Swedish Academy or over the fact that her husband's headmastership was not renewed—it is all trivial, literary proud flesh, which has nothing to do with art.[33]

Gyllensten does not mean that an author should not use personal experiences and feelings in his art. On the contrary, his repudi ation of realism implies that a writer is forced to work from himself in interpreting reality. Just as an author uses material from the reality around him in his writing, he can also make use of his own feelings as material. The difference is that his own feelings receive an objectified function in this way: they are no longer evidence of the author as a person, but carry out the significance and position which the author wishes to express in his writing. What Gyllensten rejects is art which sees an independent value in expressing the personal. In his formulations one can also read a special aversion to the auto biographical writing which lives on revelations and confessions. In the epilogue to *Det blå skeppet* (*The Blue Ship*) he em-

phatically declared that the last thing he wanted to become
was an exhibitionist (183).

Gyllensten also has a more theoretical reservation against
autobiographical writing. In an article from the beginning of
the 1950's he claimed that "the ambition to realize oneself and
to invite others to partake of this self" is not only unfruitful
but also untenable. His arguments may be summarized in the
following way: in its strictest sense the personal is characteristic
and unique. Language, on the other hand, has been formed in
a fellowship between human beings and therefore the qualities
which words denote are of a more general character. A language
which is understandable to others thus cannot express that
which is truly personal. And the result for Gyllensten was the
conclusion that "therefore egocentric or romantic ambitions are
unfruitful, seen from this point of view, and one would be
wiser to refrain from them since they only limit one's freedom
of movement without any hope of being satisfied."[34]

Hans-Erik Johannesson has demonstrated that similar thoughts
lay behind a fairly noted literary coup which Gyllensten and
one of his medical colleagues, Torgny Greitz, carried out as
early as 1946.[35] Together they wrote a collection of poems
one evening which they entitled *Camera obscura*. Their working
"method" was that one of them picked out unusual words from
textbooks and the other put them together in poems. Furthermore, they added material by means of free association. After
some hesitation the collection was accepted by Bonniers pub-
lishing house and was published under the pseudonym of Jan
Wictor. When rumors began circulating that the book was a
fake, the two authors came out into the open and revealed the
history of its creation. In a later commentary Gyllensten said
that he partly regretted their prank since it fed fuel to the
already existing conservative criticism of the modernistic poetry
of the writers of the 1940's. However, the two authors had a
serious purpose at the same time. By getting a meaningless
collection of poetry published they wished to draw attention
to the element of incomprehensibleness of the poetry of the
1940's. They especially noted such an extreme subjectivism that
communication between author and reader no longer functioned.[36] In the debate which followed, several critics stated

that a few of the poems were, in fact, fairly good, but in retrospect *Camera obscura* primarily bears witness to Gyllensten's earnest involvement long before his real debut in aesthetic questions.

It ought to be said that the definitions of realism and auto-biographical writing which Gyllensten used as a point of departure for his criticism imply stricter claims than what is usual. Not all realistic writers claim to relate reality objectively in his strict sense. And there are authors who work auto-biographically without attempting to communicate that which is uniquely personal, but who rather wish to present their own experiences because they find them representative. It is as if Gyllensten drove the goals of both realistic and autobiographical literature to their extremes. However, this "extremism" is due to the fact that his epistemological views are always a part of his aesthetic reasoning. The core of his epistemological views is that all knowledge and experience are born in the dialectic process between the individual on the one side and the reality surrounding him on the other. In this process subject and object are equally necessary. What is characteristic of Gyllensten is that he drives both realism and autobiographical writing each to its own pole in this process. For him, realism becomes a form of writing which places all its emphasis on the object and loses the subject. In contrast, autobiographical writing emphasizes the subject at the cost of the object. From his position both of these alternatives must be rejected as untenable. Instead, his own epistemological views pointed him in the direction of an aesthetics which neither lost the subject nor the object, but rather regarded literary creativity as a process in which both the writer and his surroundings are included. Consequently he viewed writing as an alloy made up of subjective and objective.

How then, can an author work more concretely, according to Gyllensten? In several of his program articles he has made comparisons between scientific research and the work of a writer, and there is hardly any doubt that his own medical research has had a strong influence on the basic program of his writing. Gyllensten has developed these thoughts most extensively in "Ordning och provokation" ("Order and Provocation"), first published in 1962, an essay the importance of which he demonstrated two years later by using it as the introductory essay in a collection entitled *Nihilistiskt credo* (*Nihilistic Credo*). "Order and Provocation" is in form a dialogue between Gyllensten the researcher and Gyllensten the author. Provoked by the author, the researcher describes his way of looking at his work. All knowledge begins with chaos, he claims; everything new is "a mess of unclear impressions and disconnected observations." In order to organize these chaotic impressions, the researcher formulates a theory or model which summarizes the observations he finds most important. The theory is then tested against a broader sector of reality and new observations can either confirm the theory or disagree with it. In the latter case the researcher is forced to alter his theory or begin again from the beginning and formulate a new theory. Gyllensten the researcher sees a tension between order and provocation throughout the whole of this process. On the one side is the will "to organize experience and tame nature, to systematize, confirm and describe finally, once and for all, how things are"—a will which, however, can lead to dogmatism and sterility. On the other side is "curiosity and the joy of discovery which want to learn more and more, experience new things, try new things and which attempt to provoke nature into revealing riches and regularities which were unknown before"—an attempt which, however, runs the risk of becoming an unplanned involvement in any number of things. In other words, both order and provocation are necessary.

To this viewpoint, Gyllensten the author replies that the researcher's description of his scientific work, with a few small alterations, fits in well with what is implied in being an author. He points out that he too wishes to "organize the world" and to "find a meaning" in the things he meets. The difference is that he himself works with a different language:

I form narrative characters and test them, ways of relating, expressions, patterns of experience, ideas, emotions, stages of life, points of view, reactions, all the stuff which fills and colors a human being and which is usually called his personality, his attitude toward life, his viewpoints and other such things. I attempt to create distinct figures and to develop them as far as I am able, to see what sinks and what floats.[37]

Of the three terms which Gyllensten the author tests to summarize his list of everything which "fills" human beings, "attitude toward life" is probably the most inclusive and just. Thus his literary program can be more concisely expressed in the following way: in his books he wants to design and test different attitudes toward life. However, it is important not to interpret this formulation too intellectually: attitudes must be understood as including both ideas and emotions. Attitudes have one aspect of "viewpoints"—philosophies of life, ideologies, and theories of the nature of reality. But another aspect of attitude has to do with "personality" and everything it implies about specific experiences and reactions. It is also important that ideas and emotions are not seen as isolated from one another. There is, in Gyllensten's epistemological view, a continual interplay in a human being between his experiences and his ideas and the attitudes he wishes to model and test ought to be regarded as products of this interplay.

Two other terms which Gyllensten also used to formulate the goals for his authorship can further illustrate the type of attitudes he wishes to work with. In the early program article "Positioner och propositioner" ("Positions and Propositions") he described his authorship as "a kind of role-taking, writing in stages."[38] With the concept "stages" he gave an important reference to Kierkegaard's great work *Stadier paa Livets Vei* (*Stages on Life's Way*). But he also opened the door on a perspective over time: stages may be said to be attitudes which follow each other in an age sequence or a developmental process. There was also a reference in Gyllensten's use of role-taking: in "Positions and Propositions" he declared that by role he meant "an attitude determined by a behavioural pattern, approximately as many social psychologists imply the term."[39] From the concept of role in its social psychological meaning it becomes further clear that it is the personal in a special sense that Gyllensten wishes to work with: attitudes, reactions, patterns. But the reference to social psychology probably also implies that he sees the roles in which he is interested as shaped in a definite social environment and as culturally conditioned. To take these roles as an author and play them out means therefore to test the ways of relating and patterns of reactions

which are current and meaningful in the society surrounding
him. For the sake of simplicity I will speak only of attitudes
toward life from now on, but the term also includes the special
denotations of "stage" and "role."

However, to understand fully Gyllensten's literary striving, it
is, of course, not sufficient to describe his scientific education
alone. In my opinion his goals must be seen against the background of "the bankruptcy of naïveté" as a whole. As I have
attempted to illustrate, "the bankruptcy of naïveté" was in
many respects a crisis. It was not only the great political
ideologies which seemed to have collapsed, but other established philosophies of life as well. Self-evident authorities were
gone and the private individual no longer had anything to cling
to. Gyllensten's literary program may be seen as a *response* to
this situation. It should be emphasized that his striving to a
great extent must be understood as a crisis program. The goal
of designing and testing different attitudes toward life expresses
a need for lying low. This is no offensive program which is
based on and preaches for any definite ideology or conviction.
To investigate different attitudes toward life means instead to
feel one's way along on shaky ground and this suggests the
work of an author with a relentlessly searching mind. The very
point of departure is a strong sense of being lost and feeling
uncertain. But in a situation where all ideologies and philosophies
of life seemed to have gone bankrupt, this program nevertheless
presented a possibility for carrying on. In his authorship
Gyllensten tests that method of dealing with "the bankruptcy of
naïveté" which, in the epilogue to *Modern Myths*, he describes
as "holding oneself by the hand and wandering on" (168).

Against the background of "the bankruptcy of naïveté" it also
becomes clear that Gyllensten's program includes two ambitions
which, although they interact, are nevertheless separate. In
"Order and Provocation" Gyllensten claimed that scientific work
has two sides: on the one hand the testing of given hypotheses
and on the other the formulation of new hypotheses. In a
corresponding way Gyllensten's literary program has both a
"destructive" and a "constructive" side. Testing different attitudes
toward life means on the one hand exposing already existing and
established attitudes to critical investigation. This means con-

cretely that common attitudes and patterns are designed and given form in such a way that it becomes clear where they are faulty and no longer viable. Here criticism dominates. But designing and testing attitudes toward life also means attempting to arrive at new ways of relating to life which may be more fruitful than the old. Here there is room for creativity and discovery. Gyllensten has dealt with this side of his program more closely in his article "Litterära 'experiment'" ("Literary 'Experiments'"). The quotation marks in the title derive from the fact that he definitely rejects the idea of the existence of experiments in any scientific meaning in literature. On the other hand, he seems to find a similarity between literary activity and scientific explorations, which he regards as "attempts at exploring new areas, either areas previously unknown or areas, dimensions, which have previously been inaccessible because we have not been in command of the technical resources." The experiment is the test of a previously formulated hypothesis, but exploration means going into the unknown with less definite intentions and expectations. Gyllensten is of the opinion that the writer, in a similar way, has an idea "of what he wants to do, in which direction he wishes to develop his possibilities, how he wishes to seek, and what he wishes to point out, etc." This idea cannot be compared with a scientific hypothesis, but like exploration, it can pave the way for new perspectives and insights:

It can still lead to important new results and discoveries—new ways of feeling, of seeing existence and interpreting it, a new sensitivity, a richer language and a richer productivity, another form of contact between human beings.[40]

How this will to critical testing can agree and interact with this striving to discover new things becomes clear in a commentary which Gyllensten wrote with regard to his novel *Senatorn* (*The Senator*). There he primarily emphasizes the fact that *The Senator* is a didactic novel which wants to illustrate that the protagonist, Antonin Bhör, goes completely astray. He describes his attitude toward Antonin Bhör and his attitude toward life more precisely in the following way:

But the person, Senator Antonin Bhör, is only the last man in the short line of romantic heroes, which I have created in the eager pedagogue's most naive conviction that he is always right in relation to his disciples and knows the nature of things. The senator must leave—he has behaved in an unsuitable manner. The senator leaves—it is after all a didactic novel, with a pedagogical moral.

Here it is the critic and pedagogue who speaks. But immediately afterward Gyllensten asks himself whether his attitude toward Antonin Bhör is only that of the superior schoolmaster. His reply is definite: "No—and that is why I write." While working on the book the critical intention functioned as a framework, but within this framework there is room for surprises:

He who writes does not only move pawns according to a scheme, he also experiences things, is surprised and altered. He receives something to remember, like someone who has taken a trip. Wenn jemand eine Reise tut, so kann er was erzählen—and, when someone writes a book, he gets something to relate.[41]

It would probably be correct to see Gyllensten's literary program primarily as a response to a profoundly experienced crisis. But it is important to emphasize that it is also a program which is open for new discoveries and new possibilities for life. If writing has been a means for Gyllensten to meet a crisis, it has also clearly been a tempting adventure for him.

VI *"Master Kierkegaard"*

By degrees Gyllensten acquired an extensive acquaintance with literature, and several Swedish and European authors gave him important inspiration during different phases of his work. But it remains obvious that one author above all others decisively influenced the formation of the whole of his writing: the Danish philosopher and author, Søren Kierkegaard. Gyllensten published an essay on him as early as 1949 which bears witness to the fact that contact with Kierkegaard's work was almost a revelation to him. In form the essay is a pastiche on Kierkegaard's method of including allegedly authentic diaries and letters in his books. To begin with Gyllensten announces that he has found a diary in a desk drawer which he calls A's diary. The entry from September 2 reads laconically "Søren Kierkegaard has made all future writing unnecessary." The author of the diary has just read the Danish doctor Hjalmar Helweg's psychological study of Kierkegaard's life; and the extensive quotations from Kierkegaard's writings and diaries have made a profound impression upon him. The depth of his experience is not only due to the fact that he has come in contact with a brilliant author, but also to the fact that what he read took a direct hold on his own experiences and thought: "Kierkegaard's problems, as he understood them, coincided so much with his own." But there is also something threatening in this extreme identification. After having read *Either—Or* and some other things, A has avoided plunging into Kierkegaard's writing "for fear of becoming like him" and because he "thought it was a good idea to have a self oneself."[42] In another essay Gyllensten has written that he had discovered Kierkegaard while he was in high school, thanks to Helweg's book;[43] and to judge from this, A expresses Gyllensten's own feelings. Evidence of this also lies in the fact that the essay is both in its form and in its ideas saturated with Kierkegaard: there is an obvious fascination both for the questions he deals with in his writing and for his methods of dealing with these questions. It is certainly correct to state that Gyllensten early felt himself to be a kindred spirit with Kierkegaard and that he later bore his authorship with him during the years he attempted to develop his own writing. A's story was also Gyllensten's even in its continuation, at times Kierkegaard came so close to him that he was forced to turn away from him for a while in order to develop his own possibilities.

Several of Gyllensten's other essays also attest to the lasting impression which Kierkegaard made on him: Gyllensten has written more about Kierkegaard than about any other author and he has often directly referred to himself as Kierkegaard's disciple. I believe one could say that Kierkegaard's significance for his writing lies on several different levels. Kierkegaard's philosophic and ironic prose style must have influenced Gyllensten, and he has to a significant extent taken up ideas and motifs from Kierkegaard's writing in his own novels. But even more important is the fact that Kierkegaard was a model for Gyllensten on a fundamental aesthetic level. In all of his essays on Kierkegaard one finds the theme of his engagement in the latter's method of presenting different possibilities for life or stages of life with the help of fictive but allegedly existing authors as pseudonyms. Gyllensten is perhaps most explicit in an amusingly subtle essay entitled "Intervju med pseudonymen 'Sören Kierkegaard'" ("Interview with the Pseudonym 'Søren Kierkegaard'"). The very method Gyllensten uses shows how close he feels to Kierkegaard. In his fantasy he conjures up Kierkegaard in his living room and they exchange opinions on each other's writing. When "Master Kierkegaard" declares that he as an author stands behind his pseudonyms without being any of them, Gyllensten replies,

I love you when you say what you are saying—I listen to you and my ears grow like leaves of lettuce in the August rain, because I have treated myself to these thoughts ever since my youth, because they are so well suited to my own intentions and hopes and they give me more strength to develop the kind of writing which I have always had in mind—my own life as an author, the experimental and exemplary vicarious life, which is good enough for him who does not wish to forget that "Truth" constantly changes guise with "Prejudice" and that reality has set up household with the caprices of art.[44]

It is important to stress that Gyllensten adopted the basic method of Kierkegaard's writing from the very beginning. In an article from 1955 he stated that Kierkegaard appealed to the individual and continued, "he appealed in such a way that he described the extreme consequences of the different possibilities, in his opinion, open to human beings to form their lives."[45] It was surely no coincidence that Gyllensten, in a questionnaire from 1958 asking which books had meant most to him, included two works of Kierkegaard in which this method is most obvious and unadulterated: in both *Either—Or* and *Stages on Life's Way* the aesthetic form of life is juxtaposed against the ethical as antithetic alternatives and in the latter work a religious form also emerges. Similarly, Gyllensten early emphasized that Kierkegaard's method led to an authorship which must be regarded as more integrated than others: "The aesthetic and the ethical are not invalidated in the religious. The excitement of his writing does not lie in the synthesis alone, but in the integrity of thesis, antithesis, and synthesis—in the figure, the tri-tone."[46] It is remarkable to see how well this method of writing fits in with Gyllensten's epistemological ideas and his view of scientific research. Kierkegaard must have been a brilliant example to Gyllensten of how a fictional author can work from the positions he himself had arrived at, and it is not strange that Kierkegaard struck him as a revelation. Everything points to the fact that he very consciously modeled his authorship along Kierke-gaard's lines.

Still, Gyllensten did not take over a perfected literary method from Kierkegaard; he also modified it according to his own needs. Kierkegaard's attempts to formulate clearly the different forms of life that he could see correspond to Gyllensten's at-tempts at testing and forming the different possibilities for life in his times, and Kierkegaard's tendency to oppose the aesthetic and ethical stages antithetically recurs in Gyllensten's method of placing different books in his own canon as theses and antith-eses to each other. Along with Kierkegaard, Gyllensten has also insisted more and more that all of his writing constitutes and ought to be read as a whole. But there is also another form of dialectics in Gyllensten's writing which ought to be referred back to his views on the nature of scientific research. The dialectics of Kierkegaard's writing may be said to have a definite endpoint: they begin in the aesthetic stage, continue into the ethical stage and have as their goal a religious form of life. Gyllensten, however, has strongly emphasized that his writing will never be completed in that way. New experiences are always here, problems can always be tackled from new points of departure and his writing is therefore in principle "an infinite inquiry"[47] to use Peirce's term. Gyllensten has sketched a striking picture of these dialectics in his novel *Diarium Spir-ituale*: "The spiral movement—circling like a hawk in rising and falling spirals over the same area, over the places where the prey lies, returning to similar motifs and tones of voice time after time, on a new level" (160). On the one hand the significance of the image is that Gyllensten moves over the same area: he is concerned with certain definite problems to which he constantly returns. But on the other hand he always continues his work on the problem and adopts new positions and attitudes time and again in his books. It especially seems as though the complications and contrasts in the positions he has already taken drive him on to seek and find new solutions. Each new work thus becomes a contribution to a discussion which is continuous.

These dialectics may well be the most significant characteristic of Gyllensten's work, and it is they which give it its special character. In a way the dialectics are the motor of his writing: they create the dynamics and vitality of Gyllensten's work as an author. And it is also these dialectics which most profoundly tie the individual works to the whole, which Gyllensten, in a representative commentary, characterized in the following way:

Actually, I don't write books—I try to construct an authorship. The individual books ought to be able to stand for themselves—but they are also part of a whole. They converse with each other and polemize against each other, they complement each other and illuminate each other. I want my books to generate a common field of forces, which originates through their mutual consensus and contrasts.[48]

To follow this continual discussion work for work is not only a way of reading which corresponds to the construction of the authorship, but also an exciting and profound adventure.

CHAPTER 2

A Dialectic Trilogy

IT is important to keep in mind that Gyllensten's novels are parts of a whole in a more solid and conscious way than is the case of most authors. But this does not mean that it is impossible to distinguish different stages or phases in his work. It is possible to divide Gyllensten's production into three periods on the basis of form. The first period includes his first book *Modern Myths* (1949), the novels *The Blue Ship* (1950), and *Barnabok* (*Infantilia*, 1952) and the small book of prose, *Carnivora* (1953). These books are very different from one another, and the period as a whole may be seen as a young author's attempts with different forms. But Gyllensten writes in the first person in both *The Blue Ship* and *Infantilia* and also to a fairly great extent in *Modern Myths*. The second period is far more homogeneous, consisting of *Senilia* (1956), *The Senator* (1958), and *Sokrates död* (*The Death of Socrates*, 1960). He has left the first person in all of these novels and instead uses an openly and ironically narrating third person. His collection of short stories, *Desperados* (*Desperadoes*, 1962), also belongs with these novels. The third period is characterized by the fact that Gyllensten works with a kind of collage method, which means that he constructs his books with the help of texts which are in part very different. This period includes all of his production after *The Death of Socrates*: *Kains memoarer* (*Cain's Memoirs*, 1963), *Juvenilia* (1965), *Diarium Spirituale* (1968), *Palatset i parken* (*The Palace in the Park*, 1970), *Grottan i öknen* (*The Cave in the Desert*, 1973), *I skuggan av Don Juan* (*In the Shadow of Don Juan*, 1975), the lyrical prose book *Lotus i Hades* (*Lotus in Hades*, 1966), and the philosophical book *Människan djuren all naturen* (*Man, Animals, All of Nature*, 1971). A destructive and liberating phase can be distinguished in this collage-period which is then followed by reconstructive work on a new foundation.

43

However, these three different periods do not only signify formal delimitations in Gyllensten's production. The novel *Senilia* also forms a turning point in his work in a deeper way: a venture from new positions in order to deal with the questions which occupied him in the earlier books. The new lines of attack were then continued in *The Senator* and *The Death of Socrates*. In the same way *Cain's Memoirs* and *Juvenilia* once again signify a new turning point in his writing, and their attempts at finding a solution are later further developed in the immediately following books. Throughout the whole of his work there is an exciting interplay between the form of the books and the ideas they present. First of all, it seems as if Gyllensten has felt that the narrative methods he has used in his previous books have bound him to the positions he has taken in them. Therefore, in order to go further with the questions which occupied him he found it necessary to search for new forms. Secondly, the new narrative methods and the new attempts at solutions have clearly emerged in a close interdependence, and they also mutually condition each other in the novels. The form itself expresses, so to speak, the ideas which are presented in the books. Therefore the formal division into periods also serves the purpose of making the dialectics of Gyllensten's production clear. By using the three periods I have mentioned as points of departure, it is possible to get a concrete idea of the dialectic movement which goes throughout the whole of his authorship.

I *Living without Involvement*

Gyllensten made his real debut relatively late: he was 27 years old when *Modern Myths* was published. Of course, it was not easy to make a beginning after a hoax such as *Camera obscura*; and the book seems to be somewhat forcedly reserved, especially in the epilogue. Still, *Modern Myths* is in many ways a remarkable opening for Gyllensten's work. It is not only that the debut was well-prepared—the texts in the book give the impression of having originated over a period of several years. It is more surprising that Gyllensten's sphere of thought already existed to such a great extent in his first book—though often in embryonic form. In *Modern Myths* it is actually possible to find approaches to many of the important ideas and motifs which he would take up in his subsequent books. To give only one example: the image of the world as a Tower of Babel, which is central throughout his authorship, can be found, fully executed, in one of the book's most important short stories (134). Furthermore, in *Modern Myths* Gyllensten was already working with different styles in a way which predicted the many different types of styles of his authorship as a whole. With the book's strongly Kierkegaardian subtitle—"Dialectic Fantasia"—he also gave a hint that he wished to see his authorship in the spirit of Kierkegaard. Finally, the point of departure for *Modern Myths* was expressly "the bankruptcy of naïveté" and the whole book was a very conscious attempt at formulating a way of meeting this situation.

Modern Myths consists of three sections. First there is a collection of aphorisms followed by about twenty poems and finally a number of stories of varying length. The basic tone of the book is, however, ironic throughout. In a foreword Gyllensten characterizes the Dutch medieval painter Hieronymus Bosch as a clown who rejects each of his canvases individually. In this way Bosch becomes an ironist who is always reserved and who only comes to life in the whole series of his reservations (7 cont.). It is clear that it is in this sense that the attitude in *Modern Myths* is most profoundly ironic, and in general Bosch functions as a kind of mentor in the book. But the irony is also directed at different contemporary ideas and conceptions which Gyllensten discards as pure myth. He is especially sharp with those who arrogantly believe they have a monopoly on the truth and with all glib attempts at seeing the world as the best possible of all worlds. Above all he has a sharp eye for the inflated rhetoric with which official truths are preached. When it comes to the point, reality is very difficult to capture. What is true from one point of view is false from another, he writes in one characteristic aphorism (24).

But behind the irony lies hot anger and the question is whether it is not this anger which gives the irony its sharpness. It is an anger which is directed both at the conditions of life and at the situation in the world. One bitter aphorism reads, "No sparrow falls to the earth without His will. And by that we have been comforted!" (21). For Gyllensten, on the contrary, the poverty and misery of the world are so obtrusive that all explanations become empty words. He has special difficulties in accepting death. In a paraphrase from the Bible he writes that the good shepherd watches over his animals from morning till evening. He protects them from poisonous leaves, unclean water, and wild animals. But that is not all: "When the time is nigh the good shepherd shall also slaughter his animals" (21). Suffering and death are everywhere the reality which shatters the myths.

But the anger in *Modern Myths* is especially directed at everything artificial and conventional in our culture. In the expressionistically colored short story, "Tango jalousie," life is described as a boisterous dance in a crowded restaurant. The provocative music, the chattering people, tuxedoes, the women's powder, the drinks, the vomit—all create an intense atmosphere of stuffiness and disgust. Perhaps there is also at bottom a feeling of disappointment in life. Another short story tells about a young man who falls in love with a seemingly innocent young girl. But one day a dirty old man offers to sell him some pornographic pictures and they show the girl photographed from the most immodest angle. The story does not have the same ironic defenses as the other stories in *Modern Myths* and therefore seems unusually direct and open.

How, then, can the individual relate to the entangling conventions which surround him/her? "Livet i salongerna" ("Life in the Parlors") answers that question in a way which practically parodies the Existentialists' philosophical theses. A person comes into a parlor where there is a group consisting of a couple of ladies and gentlemen. They are occupied with drinking good port wine and eating almond cakes. When the new arrival appears in the door all eyes turn to him, and he thus finds himself in a situation which demands that he do something. Since the parlor is ridiculous he could place himself outside of its rules and regulations. But then he runs the risk of being dismissed as a fool. He could become a musician and spin a well-tempered fugue around his pain. But the fugue must be spun in the parlor anyway, so the problem of how he should behave himself remains. Perhaps he could silence his experience

of the ridiculousness of the parlor in the belief that it is
an inadequate experience. Or perhaps he should leap out of
the parlor and into some kind of love affair—here Gyllensten
clearly has Kierkegaard's leap of faith in mind. But these possibilities are also rejected. The leap is too risky: there are so
many gods that one could become a Nazi just as easily as a
Pentecostalist. The only remaining solution is to accept the
situation instead and to live without seriousness. One must
simply go into the parlor and play the game according to the
rules: deal out compliments to the ladies (but no kisses), sip
the port wine (not too much, however), eat the almond cakes
(without smacking one's lips) and passionlessly take part in
the conversation on the fashion of ties or morality or a prima
donna or other nonsense.

This attitude toward life is further developed in the suggestive
story "Kvinnotornet" ("The Tower of Women"). A man has
built a tower seven stories high on an island in the Stockholm
archipelago. On six of the floors he keeps six different women
whom he visits in turn during the six week-days. The women
are described in great detail, but at the same time it is clear
that they represent different forms of living and life-situations.
The man also partially changes guise depending on whom he
is with. The first woman is indolent, buxom and sleepy. The
cushions, drapes, rugs—everything in her room is soft and
smooth. With her he can sink into a soothing soft sensuousness
and surrender his individuality. She is peace and rest. The
next woman in turn is a totally different type. She is thin,
with shaved legs, and on her forehead no blemish has ever
made its mark. In her air-conditioned room she is busy quickly
typing the final draft of a scientific article. The man dances a
comradely tango with her and afterward they each shower
by themselves. She is the pure intellect without feelings—or
with atrophied feelings. The other women in the tower are
also very different from each other. The man has fallen for the
third woman for the sake of her eyes. From her he learns the
eye's peaceful and profound joy: the art of regarding the world
without desiring it. The fourth woman is middle-aged and
heavy, and she welcomes him with curlers in her hair. Their
life together is one of faithful habit and they have a thousand

and three children. The fifth woman is the young daughter of a minister and together with her the man experiences again and again lost innocence. The sixth woman, finally, is the most grotesque of the man's women. With an old lady's fat, swollen body and a seventeen-year-old girl's fragile face she scrubs the man so that blood flows and gives him soothing kisses at the same time. Perhaps she represents both the beauty of the body and its unavoidable decay.

The man receives some different kind of pleasure from each of these women, and he visits them in turn week after week. But on Sundays he goes down to the beach, lies naked in the warm sand, and in a way throws off the women for whom he now feels disgust and shame. The whole of this ritual pattern of action can be seen as a polemic parallel to the Bible's story of creation. The man who is in full activity six days in his tower and who then rests on the seventh almost appears as a fellow competitor to our creator! In this religious perspective the point of view the story presents becomes clearer: God does not exist and therefore there is no single, absolute and correct way of living either; but human beings can still create their own existences. Seen more closely, the tower of women demonstrates a way of living which implies testing many different forms of life. One could claim that the man's goal is to exploit all the possibilities life offers. But at the same time it is clearly very important that he turns his back on his women every Sunday, and it seems that the main point is to remain free and not tied down deep inside. He curses and ridicules his women individually and finds the individual forms of living they represent arbitrary and insufficient. But he finds a value in his fidelity to the whole series of them. Here it becomes obvious that the man in the tower of women practices an attitude toward life which corresponds to the introductory character sketch of Hieronymus Bosch as an ironist who always has reservations.

Modern Myths is sub-titled "Dialectic Fantasia" with very good reason: the book is filled with tension and supplies no easy answers. In both "Life in the Parlors" and "The Tower of Women" an almost repugnant repudiation of reality lies close at hand. With its swarming life in all conceivable forms

the world seems grotesque and existence without real meaning—
it is not for nothing that Gyllensten calls the tower of women
a tower of Babel (134). In the fury with which the man in
the tower devotes himself to his women there is also a touch
of despair. Several other stories bear witness to the same thing.
In "Poetens giftermål" ("The Marriage of the Poet") he asks
whether the clown's freedom is not in fact an incapacity for
love. "Balladen om alla flammor, jag aldrig kysst" ("The Ballad
of all the Flames I never Kissed") describes the attraction to
a stronger and more immediate love: three generals each exercises his own huge army of words, but at the same time is
attracted to a young girl who asks nothing more than to be
able to say everything to her lover. And in "Skriket" ("The
Scream"), there is both the longing for and the fear of being
violently and inexorably marked by life. All of these approaches
point toward *The Blue Ship.*

Still there is no doubt that in the end Gyllensten is in favor
of the attitude toward life which is formulated in "Life in the
Parlors" and "The Tower of Women." *Modern Myths* as a
whole forms itself into a plea for what he in the epilogue calls
a conscious and conviction-less form of life, which means that
the individual creates his reality every minute as in a game
(171). It is quite acceptable to live without either involvement or faith, he claims; in fact, it is the only respectable
alternative. It is not only that he cannot find any especially
true or valid conviction among those for sale. In the epilogue
he also emphasizes more emphatically than previously in the
book, that involvement easily becomes fanaticism and aggression
(170). He already touched on that theme in "Life in the
Parlors": it is said that the man in the parlor is certainly no
lover, but he is not a murderer either (93). But this rejection
of all dangerous convictions and adventures becomes most clear
in the prayer to the every-day, which, together with the epilogue,
concludes *Modern Myths.* Characteristically, the prayer is a
polemical paraphrase of the Lord's Prayer and expresses a
striving to live a simple, ordinary, every-day life:

Great day
which resides in our hands!

Hallowed be thy labor
Give us thy toil
Fill up our time
on earth as it is on the seas!
Give us this day our daily striving
and give us new debts
so that even tomorrow is filled with tasks
and lead us not into loneliness
but deliver us from ourselves.
For thine is the earnestness and the strength and the reality
in all of our lives. (167)

But at the same time one might characterize this conviction-less attitude as a kind of heroic attitude of the type which also emerged elsewhere in the literature after World War II. In this respect I think that *Modern Myths* is especially close to Albert Camus's *Le mythe de Sisyphe* (*The Myth of Sisyphus*, 1942).[1] Camus's point of departure was suicide, which was in his opinion the only truly serious philosophical problem. Thrown into an existence which is experienced as absurd, the human being finally asks himself about the meaning of life: seen concretely, is life worth living or not? Camus gave his reply to that question in his interpretation of the figure of Sisyphus, who, according to the myth, received as his punishment from the gods the task of pushing a huge rock up a hill only to see it roll back down again every time. In Sisyphus Camus saw the absurd hero. Sisyphus is, he claimed, totally aware of the fruitlessness of his exertions: he knows that the rock will always roll back down again. But with a relentless expression he pushes the rock up the hill again and again. He defies the absurd with all of his might and finds his happiness in doing so. It is a question of heroism of gigantic format, which means that he challenges the whole of existence.

There are several interesting points of contact between *Modern Myths* and *The Myth of Sisyphus*. Camus's view of existence as absurd corresponds to Gyllensten's experience of the world as conventional and artificial. Like Camus, Gyllensten maintains this basic experience and does not allow himself to be tempted by more reconcilable views. But above all the attitude toward life expressed in *Modern Myths* is relentless and hard-won in a way which bears striking resemblance to Camus's interpretation of the myth of Sisyphus. In "Life in the Parlors" and "The Tower of Women" there is an especially strong emotional resistance to the world of hollow conventions which meets the human being. Both of the protagonists long for something else, but there are no other possibilities in sight. In this situation it is easy to become resigned, but instead Gyllensten lets them use their wills to play the game in the world which actually exists. His is a more everyday kind of heroism than Camus's, but to a great extent it is a question of enduring—perhaps in the hope that something else will present itself. Therefore it is hardly surprising that Gyllensten would try out totally new lines of attack in his next book.

II *Betting on the Miracle*

With *The Blue Ship* Gyllensten deliberately offered an alternative to *Modern Myths* and presented an attitude toward life which was a direct antithesis to the possibility of living without involvement. The difference is clear from the language alone. The open and strong, emotionally charged language of *The Blue Ship* is in contrast to the ironic intellectual style of *Modern Myths*; and as Gyllensten himself pointed out in a note to the book, he characteristically took up a terminology which was used by the Romantics. The scene of the novel is the steamboat *Forward Roll*, which glides through Stockholm's glittering archipelago and lands at its numerous docks. But the description of the boat also has ties to the medieval view of the world: the captain, enthroned on the bridge on top, represents God, the crew are the people on earth, and the stokers in the glowing engine room are in hell. Perhaps it is also a Romantic trait that the protagonist Abraham is a young innocent boy who has not yet really made his debut into the world. The action of the book is that he investigates the different parts of the boat and is confronted by the crew aboard. The crew share their experiences with him in a series of stories which they each tell him in turn. Abraham's mother is also aboard the boat, as the cook. She bears the soft name Emma, and she also tells Abraham stories. There is high and obvious tension throughout the book between Emma and the other members of the crew.

The mystical, unapproachable captain on the bridge commands the whole crew. No one really knows what he is like and he appears in different guises in the crew's stories—just as human beings have created different images of God. Sometimes he is a fiery and drunken skipper, sometimes he assumes grotesque forms. The only time Abraham sees him he is a naked bundle, who smells sour and dirty. One half of his body is an old man's, the other an old lady's; and the figure is immobile except for the trembling arms which clumsily caress their own body. Right in the middle of the fancy new captain's hat is a message which reads: "Divil" and "Ass" (101). Though the captain assumes different guises, he is always presented as an evil god. In one of the mate's stories he behaves like a loud and enthusiastic hunter. But what for a long time seems to be an ordinary hunt in the end reveals itself to be a hunt for human children! The implication of the story is that God is a killer and a doer of misdeeds. The other members of the crew also bear witness in different ways that creation is evil. The steersman tells how he lost both his parents while very young and thereafter was forced to live as an unwelcome child in his uncle's family. The three stokers' stories also deal with early disappointments which changed life into a torment for them: the first of them felt his heart explode when he saw his mother together with a lover, the second cannot forget that his father forced himself on his mother through blackmail and that she hated him for it, and the third has discovered that he has difficult emotional disturbances in relation to women. These experiences have filled them with hate, and in the engine room they stoke the fire with pieces of flesh which they tear from each other's bodies. Gyllensten has also established a link with Hieronymus Bosch in *The Blue Ship*, here primarily to his pictures of life on earth as hellish and grotesque.

Together they are a motley crew, but they all have the same attitude to the ship's evil world. Gyllensten gave *The Blue Ship* a motto from the German author Sebastian Brant's medieval epic poem *Das Narrenschiff* (*The Ship of Fools*) and he presents the crew as fools. In the absence of the captain they pour the vilest of curses upon him, but when his voice gives orders through the speaker tube they jump to it like marionettes and carry out his commands. In spite of the fact that they reject the conditions aboard with all their hearts, they almost find honor in following orders. Their foolishness lies in keeping a straight face in an evil game: they resignedly let the ship carry them where it will. But in doing so their existence loses its reality and they are transformed into shadow-like beings. A recurrent image is that the features of the crew are obliterated as if someone had gone over them with an eraser: by not being true to their feelings their personalities disintegrate and they end up in a death-like emptiness. The crew's situation becomes especially clear in a lyrical dialogue between Emma and the steersman. When she asks him how long he is going to drift around and why he never finds the right way, he can only answer, "With my dry eyes I cannot cry. How can listless eyes smile? My bloodless lips can never kiss. Wilted lips cannot pray" (86). Dry eyes, bloodless lips, and faded skin—these are the outer signs of an inner emptiness which is characteristic of all the crew.

The greatest of fools, however, is an affected little dwarf who, as a person, in many ways summarizes the crew's attitude toward life. He calls himself Professor Cherubini, is a master in the Black Magic of Yama and is in complete command of the art of conquering pain. He trained himself to endure uncomfortable positions as a child, and later he learned to stick pins through practically all of the parts of his body. Now he is in complete command of his body: it feels no suffering and obeys him like a slave. The trick is only that he surrender himself to the ocean of indifference which exists inside of him. By giving up all striving and ambition he arrives at total freedom. He gives nothing and takes nothing, he stands outside and looks on. There is no doubt that this remarkable act by and large corresponds to the attitude toward life which is presented in *Modern Myths*. But this time it is presented in a characteristically pointed form: the possibility of living without involvement has become the art of living with no feelings at all. Professor Cherubini does not feel the pins he sticks into his body, and in the same way he lives only in appearance. In reality he is a person who wishes at any price to prevent life from touching him.

In one of the strongest scenes in *The Blue Ship*, Professor Cherubini demonstrates his feat for Emma and Abraham. He presents himself dressed in blue silk trousers with spangles in the light of a flickering candle. With a high forced voice he allows each movement to be preceded by an incantation and then poses for the public. He begins by sticking pins into the creases under his chin and into his cheeks, continues with the earlobes, neck, thighs, and hands, and concludes by driving an especially long thin pin into the right side of his stomach— in the end he is prickly as a porcupine. The purpose of Professor Cherubini's performance is to win Emma and Abraham to his art. He thinks he sees a promising disciple in Abraham and wants to buy him from Emma for the Judas sum of thirty crowns. But Emma is not deceived. By appealing to Professor Cherubini's vanity she gets him to drive the pin into his stomach once again, suddenly grasps him by the arms, carries him to the railing and throws him into the sea. A hissing scream is heard, and he sinks like a stone.

It is no accident that it is Emma who saves Abraham from Professor Cherubini. From the very beginning she distinguishes herself notably from the rest of the crew. To a certain extent she is a somewhat careless unwed mother who leaves her son alone too often. But seen more profoundly she becomes a very positive figure. First of all, she has a soft sensuality which is in direct contrast to the raw alcoholic orgies of the crew. Abraham has an hour of intense enjoyment every morning when he is allowed to crawl into bed with her—she fondles him and calls him the most wonderful pet names. She is "so big and full of splendid secrets," and he is also a bit afraid of her (19). Furthermore, she is the only one who really cares about Abraham for his own sake and takes care of him when it is necessary. On the whole she has not been corrupted by the existence aboard in the same way as the other members of the crew: she is free from the stunted feelings of jealousy and hate which still storm in them. Instead she is very serious in the face of life, and she also radiates a remarkable purity. It is obvious that she represents a totally different way of living than the shadow-life of the fools, as becomes especially clear in her decisive repudiation of Professor Cherubini:

I don't believe in you. Your freedom is the freedom of one who
has gone bankrupt, your freedom is only renunciation. You have
made a virtue of necessity. You are a bad artist. It is you who
are the dead god of liberty. (36)

It is in this field of tension between the fools and Emma that
Abraham moves. He becomes frightened several times by the
grotesque crew members and their gruesome stories, but he
always returns to the security of Emma to comfort himself
with her stories. Somewhat baldly it could be said that the
crew and the mother struggle for his soul and that he himself
must choose between two very different ways of living. One
beautiful morning the *Forward Roll* lies at anchor near a larger
island and Abraham goes ashore on an exploring expedition.
He is wide-open and receptive to everything he meets: he
even feels the stones, tufts, and sticks of the road through the
thin soles of his worn sneakers. He creeps quietly past a group
of boys in fear of being harassed. But outside of the island's
boarding house he meets two half-grown girls who reveal
themselves to be twins. They approach each other carefully,
build a huge harbor on the beach, swim giggling without suits,
and plunder a patch of wild strawberries. In the end both
girls declare that Abraham may kiss them good-bye. It is the
first time for all three of them, and no one really knows how.
They are shy, clumsy and afraid: "Can you get pregnant? Does
it show afterwards? What happens to you?" (160). It feels
like it takes two hours for their mouths to come close to each
other. But then Abraham sees that shadows from the branches
of the trees cross the girls' faces, and suddenly the shadows
are like dead hands. What happens to Abraham is that an
awareness of death breaks in on the light summer day, and
he reacts in the same way as the fools aboard the boat. Frightened, he draws out of the living experience and rushes away
crying. He already, however, has guilt feelings: he has an idea
that he faced the possibility of love, but failed.

Now Emma takes care of Abraham a last time. She dries
his tears and feeds him some sugar lumps dipped in brandy.
But more important is the advice she gives him. She understands that he is growing up and therefore tells him how she

met his father. When she was a girl she worked as a servant
on a large farm. She lived in an attic room and had to work
like a man. The people on the farm only spoke to her when
they wanted something done, and their hands were always fists.
They never smiled and only kissed in the dark, as if they
were ashamed. It was a farm which always lay in shadow. But
when Emma was on her way to being grown up she met a
man who was unlike any other she had met. He had open hands
full of caresses and smiling lips, and he became her lover. They
were united in the middle of a billowing rye field and found
a home "among tears and laughter and things which live and
die" (172). The profound exultation transforms Emma's story
into a piece of intensely lyrical prose.

The following morning Emma demonstrates in action the
significance of her story. She gets up earlier than usual, scrubs
the galley shining clean, washes and dresses with great care.
Abraham is with her all the time and admires her "as something
beautiful and unapproachable when one is too little and too
poor" (174). Then they go up on deck, lower one of the life-
boats and jump down into it. In the meantime the crew gather
with their bloodless faces and hang over the railing like empty
clothes. Down in the boat Emma takes off her shoes and neatly
places them on the bench. She then climbs out of the boat,
balancing carefully between the waves so that the edges do
not hurt her, and walks away from the ship of fools. With
bowed head she wanders down the sun street toward the
horizon where the sea disappears.

This is an intense and profound experience for Abraham. He
remains alone in the bottom of the lifeboat: a child crying
and becoming an adult. Now that his mother has left him he
knows that his childhood is over, and he feels a longing which
will always return. He understands that nothing will be as
it was. But Emma has also shown what it means to be grown
up. The previous night Abraham has an uneasy dream which
depicts a rite of initiation. Around the fire in the ship's engine
room he sees befeathered chiefs and a pair of youths who
are to be initiated into the mysteries. Some older men cut deep
holes in the young men's breast and back muscles, drive in
wooden sticks which are tied with ropes and lift them up

in the air. All the while the chiefs judge their ability to endure pain and their courage. It is a cruel rite, which recalls strongly the raw brutality of the fools and especially Professor Cherubini's art. But at the same time the scene points remarkably enough forward to the end filled with light. Emma's last action also has a ritual character, and the stretch from the meeting with the girls to Emma's departure is Abraham's initiation into adult life. Perhaps it is the awareness of death, above all, which makes him an adult and so frightened that he turns his back on life for a while in the way of the fools. But Emma's last story does not only say that love is possible. It also demonstrates the fact that life and death irreconcilably belong together. The fools who try to avoid death lose life at the same time, but Emma knows that he who wishes to win life must accept pain and death in the bargain. Where he lies crying in the lifeboat Abraham is alone and abandoned, but he also has the possibility to follow Emma's path away from the ship of fools.

The Blue Ship is permeated with the language and symbolism of religion. Emma's wandering over water is a true miracle which naturally leads one's thoughts to Jesus. Furthermore, behind the boy Abraham lurks the great biblical patriarch with the same name—a motif which is emphasized by another of the novel's mottoes, where it is written that the boy's story is an eternally recurring story. Gyllensten has certainly been impressed by Kierkegaard's *Fear and Trembling*, which presents the Bible's Abraham in a way which recurs in *The Blue Ship* in all its unprecedented acuteness. For Kierkegaard, Abraham's greatness lies in the fact that his faith is a faith in the power of the absurd. God commanded him to make an offering of his late-born son. When he raised the knife over Isaac he did something which is incomprehensible and unreasonable by all human measures. But his faith was so immovable that he never hesitated to obey God's command, and it was just therefore that he won back Isaac. The same emotional tension exists in *The Blue Ship.* When Emma wanders away over the water she does something which, for the fools aboard the ship, seems both unthinkable and impossible; and Abraham finds himself in a similar situation as his biblical namesake. The last chapter is subtitled "Abraham's Sacrifice" and it is clear that he must

sacrifice childhood in order to win a life in the adult world
which is still uncertain and out of his reach. As for the connection with Kierkegaard, it is to a great extent a question of
a leap into the unknown.

However, the problems raised by *The Blue Ship* do not
resolve into a religious solution. As in his later novels, Gyllensten
used religious terminology to formulate worldly problems, and
in several of his essays he has declared that he finds the religious
language very fruitful just for this purpose.[2] The ship, constructed along the lines of the medieval view of the world, is
just as much a description of the bankrupt world after the
war as *Modern Myths*. But in *The Blue Ship* the goal of living
life without involvement is seen as lack of love and courage.
The heroically striving protagonists in "Life in the Parlors"
and "The Tower of Women" have been transformed into empty
and dead fools, and their senses of guilt spring from the
suspicion that perhaps there is still another way of living. Instead
it is the soft and serious Emma who presents the novel's message
of the possibilities of love. It is important to note that this is
no facile solution. Emma is just as aware of the sufferings and
death of human beings as the fools. But instead of focusing on
that awareness she possesses the ability to devote herself to
life with all that it implies of both good and evil. One could
say that *The Blue Ship* is primarily about the courage which is
necessary for life. In the afterword Gyllensten summarized the
novel's viewpoint with the formula "bet on the miracle," and
it is clear that it is a question of a risky business with no
guarantees whatsoever. The light around the figure of Emma
springs most deeply from the fact that she dares to bet on
love as a miracle. She knows that life can kill, but acts in the
hope that love will bear it.

With *The Blue Ship* Gyllensten not only presented a counter-
offer to the attitude toward life in *Modern Myths*. As statement
and reply both books generate a strong field of tension in
relation to each other and this tension is fundamentally significant in his work. On the one hand there exists in *Modern
Myths* what one could call a striving to keep life at a distance:
a sharp criticism of contemporary events and life styles, a
profound skepticism toward established ways of thinking and

dogmas, and a solicitous care for the simple everyday life. On the other hand, *The Blue Ship* expresses a longing for greater surrender to life and advocates an attempt at finding a dynamic and meaningful existence. Gyllensten's first two books demonstrated in a remarkable way the two poles between which his future writings would move.

III   *The Murderous Child*

In a commentary on *Infantilia* Gyllensten declared that he regarded his first three books as a trilogy, and it is clear that he once again took up questions from *Modern Myths* and *The Blue Ship* in his new novel.[3] The protagonist of *Infantilia* is called Karl-Erik, a man torn between two women throughout the book. As Bertil Palmqvist has shown, these two women incarnate the two opposing attitudes toward life in *Modern Myths* and *The Blue Ship*.[4] Klem stands for the possibility of a life without involvement while Lucy represents the possibility of a much greater surrender to life. At the same time Gyllensten continues the discussion in *Infantilia* and characterizes the two alternatives in somewhat newer terms. Karl-Erik's relationship to Klem is presented as a marriage of reason, and his attraction to Lucy as a longing for really great passion. But *Infantilia* primarily deals with the conflict between both of these attitudes and with Karl-Erik's difficulties in orienting himself in the field of tension between them. This paradigm is clear in the action of the novel: Karl-Erik is first together with Klem, then abandons her to live with Lucy, returns for a second try with Klem, but is finally once again drawn to Lucy.

The novel begins, however, with a few childhood episodes which establish the book's emotional atmosphere. In retrospect Karl-Erik remembers a tight-rope walker in a visiting circus, an expedition with some other children to steal syrup, and a German boy's summer visit with the family. All of these episodes point to the central motifs in the novel: Karl-Erik attempts a balancing act between the two women, he is a typical parasite, living off others; and the German boy represents the rise of Nazism and the "bankruptcy of naïveté." But most remarkable is the childish tone of these memories. *Infantilia* is narrated in a

kind of childish spoken language with fragmented phrases and
free associations which suggestively capture childish feelings
of being abandoned, avariciousness, and jealousy. It is especially
striking that people and events are placed together in such a
way that they almost glide into each other—a technique which
Gyllensten would come to develop with even greater virtuosity
in his later work. For example, in the first chapter Miss Dassy
is both a tight-rope walker *and* a little puppy, and the circus
visit is hereby woven together with a quarrel between Karl-
Erik's parents. This childish language is continuous throughout
Infantilia, and episodes from Karl-Erik's childhood also emerge
later on to characterize events in his adult life. It is clear that
Gyllensten wishes to present Karl-Erik as a very childish person,
the subject of an infantile regression.

On the now-level of the novel Karl-Erik is about thirty years
old. He has his high-school diploma but is only occasionally
employed doing mechanical office jobs. The work means nothing
to him and can give his life no meaning. The same is true of
his relationship to Klem, into which he seems to have more
or less fallen. At first Karl-Erik and Klem form a little
gang together with Karl-Erik's friend Totte and Lucy, and
one Sunday all four of them are out on a ski trip. They take
the wrong way, it gets dark, and they break into an out-of-the-
way cottage. They light the fire, supply themselves with food
and liquor, sleep over and write at last "Thanks for us" on
the whitewashed chimney (26). The solicitously cared-for and
idyllic cottage makes the confusion and helplessness of their
lives glaringly clear. A few weeks later Karl-Erik finds a pair
of pajamas which Klem has taken from the cottage in her
drawer. He understands that the pajamas represent her dreams
of a happy marriage with him, becomes unreasonably angry, and
tears them to pieces. But later on he becomes ashamed of
himself and thinks that they live a poor life. On an outer level
this poverty is manifested in their provisory and shabby home.

Karl-Erik is also completely aware that, on his part at least,
there is no question of love in his relationship to Klem. He
stays together with her because she is the only one offered to
him and she is in any case better than nothing. But in his
erratic inner monologues there are dismal expressions of the

emptiness and isolation of his life. He feels that his hands are strangers he does not recognize. Intercourse between him and Klem is referred to in the form of a record of the skin areas which come in touch with each other: skin of the hand against the cheek and forehead, skin of the lips against skin of the throat, breast skin against thigh skin, secret skin against secret skin. The substances exchanged during intercourse are bits of skin, saliva, breath and mucous (34 cont.). The absence of love turns their sexual life into a disgusting mechanical activity. Klem calls herself Thea and thinks it means goddess, but for Karl-Erik she is the demimondaine Thais.

Therefore it is not so strange that Karl-Erik also characterizes his existence as a form of spiritual death. In expressions which are reminiscent of T. S. Eliot's *The Waste Land* he complains: "My valley is my death, my playmate is the dead one. Not a strong death, or a raw one, but a weak death, a tepid one, purified. The waste valley" (32). At the same time he believes that this dead existence is perhaps due to his lack of ability to love. He feels he cannot love Klem in the way he is meant to, and this suspicion gives him a feeling of guilt. There are many similarities between Karl-Erik and the fools in *The Blue Ship*.

Seen against this background it is hardly surprising that Karl-Erik reaches out after other possibilities than Klem. One day he wants to find Totte, but only Lucy is at home. She is strained, invites him in, and after a while she bursts out with the news that she is pregnant and that Totte has left her. Karl-Erik feels uneasy but is also attracted by the nakedness of her sorrow. He feels that perhaps she can awaken his passion, is drawn closer to her, and remains overnight. And their relationship *is* passionate—even though it is a question of fairly complex emotions. Once they make love with each other while Totte tries in vain to open the outer door, on which Karl-Erik has installed a new lock. This behavior is shameless and inordinate, exceeding anything Karl-Erik has previously experienced. Thus he is even more hurt when he learns that Lucy has given Totte the new key, and he abandons her in violent protest. This series of events is summarized when Karl-Erik recalls a blue train from a childhood visit to a carnival (54 cont.). He remembers that in the darkness of the tunnel a sign appears encouraging people to kiss, but the next minute the doors are opened and the ones who followed the directive are delivered up to the laughs of the spectators. The image symbolizes his feelings for what has happened to him: together with Lucy he has attempted surrender, but it did not work out, and he is now a ridiculous figure. Further on the experience becomes even more definite in the same terms as the imagery of the blue train: "The light always comes to me. Darkness deceives me" (67).

This light and dark symbolism is used throughout *Infantilia* to characterize both women, and the contrast between the possibilities they represent is thus thrown into even stronger relief. For Karl-Erik, living with Klem means using one's will to arrange one's life as well as possible. It is the same as a marriage of necessity. On the other hand, living with Lucy presents him with the possibility of being naked and of being swept up by something greater than himself. But above all, Lucy is associated with a life-giving darkness and Klem with a light which transforms such dreams to illusions. Toward the middle of the novel the choice between Lucy and Klem is formulated in the following suggestive way:

But if I came into a dark room and they were there gliding in the darkness. Then I would seek the one recognize her like a scent a skin my spit on her skin. Skin girl the naked one I would recognize her in the darkness and fall toward her but I would not notice the other. But if the light were turned on I would go to the other and marry her. (67)

The passion Karl-Erik experiences with Lucy has a profound grip on him. He is so surprised that such a thing could happen to him that it seems like something of a miracle: "... there were no voices around us only we and it was reckless and kind of bloody and all alone before everything else" (63). But in his disappointment that this surrender showed itself to be untenable he once again attempts to arrange his life with Klem. He knows that this decision implies a drastic reduction of his expectations: a life together with Klem is only a question of endurance. But he nevertheless attempts to build up such a life together with her and acquiesces to her dream of marriage. Their few relatives come traveling, and the wedding dinner is held outdoors. But for Karl-Erik a childhood memory cuts into the wedding ceremony. One Sunday he and some other children paired a little terrier bitch with a big mutt behind a mission chapel. Lascivious and excited by the unseemliness, they stood in a circle and viewed the performance. In some way they felt that they had desecrated a sacrament. Here it is not only Karl-Erik's disgust with regard to mechanical sexuality which is revealed. The memory also provides a measurement of his despair: he is not capable of conquering his feelings of alienation and death. Thus his marriage becomes a violation of love.

It does not take long before Karl-Erik's and Klem's marriage of reason once again begins to crack and fall apart. Karl-Erik soon sees that will alone is not enough to keep their marriage going: "One must get something, otherwise there is nothing to arrange" (80). His ambition was to eradicate Lucy from his heart once and for all, but he is unable to forget her. When the boredom in his marriage with Klem increases he begins a new movement toward Lucy. The tensions between Klem and him are focused on the question of whether or not to have children. Karl-Erik defends himself against Klem's desire for children with the view that it is an unsuitable infant sacrifice to beget children for one's own salvation. One day she comes home with a baby carriage which she has not been able to resist buying. But as in the scene with the pajamas from the cottage, Karl-Erik becomes furious and breaks the baby carriage into bits and pieces. A child himself, he obviously cannot tolerate the idea of any other child. After this violent performance he leaves Klem for good.

For Karl-Erik the break-up of his marriage is followed by an attempt at leaving his previous life completely behind him. This chapter is entitled "Jonah in the Stomach of the Whale," and like a later-day Jonah Karl-Erik lets himself sink down to the bottom of society in the hope of winning rebirth in this way. He drifts around the streets, sleeps out at night, and gets dirtier and more decrepit. On a concrete level the stomach of the whale is symbolized by the big waiting room of the Stockholm Central Station, where he comes regularly to sit in its warmth: the domed ceiling is supported by a rib-like steel construction. During this vagabond existence Karl-Erik lands in a deadly condition which is more intrusive than any he has previously experienced. In his eye the city streets are "dried out canyons" (125). A visit to his apartment makes him think of a dead man's home with himself as the corpse (136 cont.). After this death phase he is thrown up to Lucy's apartment, but in contrast to Jonah he is not reborn. Like the previous time, it is passion he seeks in Lucy. In order for them to be completely united with each other there must be no boundaries between them. Therefore he prays to her, "... suck me up destroy my body damned individual dissolve it all words will possibilities all self-will destroy it for me!" (143). But once again Lucy is involved in relationships which prevent such a total unity. According to Karl-Erik it was her hope that Totte would come back which was in the way before, and now it is the newborn baby who stands between them. And his increasing despair at not being gripped by passion is also directed toward the child. One evening he fills the bathtub with water and in an unguarded moment takes the child with him and drowns it. It is quickly done, the little body is soon limp.

How Karl-Erik appears as a child is of vital importance in interpreting *Infantilia*. There are many aspects worth noticing. In a very significant reflection upon himself Karl-Erik states, "There is a dead child somewhere in me; yes murdered, if one is not afraid of hard words and since guilt is also hidden in it" (119). There can hardly be any doubt that this expressive statement refers to "the bankruptcy of naïveté." The dead child in Karl-Erik stands for the loss of "the immediate involvement" which he has experienced. In other words he is in a situation where he has lost the ability to become involved but still cannot find himself in an existence without love. Though dead, the child within him leaves him no peace. The corpse smells, as he says (119, 146). But Karl-Erik also appears as a child in the more general sense that he is so strongly attracted to the alternative of surrender. The condition and possibilities of surrender are in general associated with children and childishness in Gyllensten's earlier books. In *The Blue Ship* it is a young boy who faces the possibility of surrendering to life.

At the same time it is clear that surrender has a darker nuance in *Infantilia*—which is underlined in the novel's light and dark symbolism. In *The Blue Ship* surrender has the character of a necessary affirmation of life, but in the surrender Karl-Erik longs for there is something pulling him toward downfall and death. The passion he seeks in Lucy is in conflict with a social life. Before his second attempt with Lucy Karl-Erik leaves his work and his apartment and several times attempts to get Lucy to refrain from working. His actions can hardly be understood other than as an expression of the idea that passion can only be realized if one turns away from society. Karl-Erik's prayer to Lucy that she destroy the "individual" in him is even more sharply anti-life. The clearly destructive terms in his prayer suggest a link between his wish for liberation from his own ego and an attraction to the annihilation of physical death. Furthermore, Karl-Erik's attraction to surrender is dangerous for others: in him the other side of passion is a violent jealousy. First Totte and then the child stands in the way of the unity he wants to achieve with Lucy and his jealousy in relation to the child is especially pronounced—from the very beginning he gives it "the evil eye" (141). In all its extremity, the formula for the passion Karl-Erik seeks in Lucy is tyrannical: only we two. But the moment he makes this demand on her, the child becomes an intruder that provokes his jealousy. Passion demands that the child be put out of the way. This violent and dangerous jealousy comprises still another important component of Karl-Erik's childishness.

The complex murder of the child is understandable in the light of Karl-Erik's childishness. Here Bertil Palmqvist has pointed out that *Infantilia* is directly tied to the final scene of *The Blue Ship*: Karl-Erik's action is a sacrifice for which Abraham the patriarch has served as a mystical pattern.[5] Karl-Erik sacrifices the child so that he and Lucy can achieve an ego-disintegrating ecstasy. But the contrast between Karl-Erik and Abraham is no less glaring than the one between Karl-Erik and Jonah. Abraham's sacrifice signified a confirmation of his union with God. Karl-Erik's sacrifice, however, leads nowhere. His action is a last desperate attempt at achieving total surrender with Lucy, but it results in nothing less than

manslaughter. It is only the confused Karl-Erik who believes
that his sacrifice has any meaning; in reality he is a murderer.
The contrast with the boy Abraham's life-affirming sacrifice
can hardly be sharper.

But the murder of the child also has another significance. In
the description of the murder it is pointed out that Karl-Erik
feels a vague connection between the dead child in him and
Lucy's child. Karl-Erik, more and more confused, is incapable
of making the distinction between his emotions and outer reality;
instead the child within him fuses with the baby in the basket.
In this perspective the murder of the child appears as Karl-
Erik's attempt to eradicate his longing for surrender. When he
drowns Lucy's child he also performs a ritual which is meant
to free him from the dead child within him—in the text there
is a strong parallel between the scene in the bath and a ritual
of purification through immersion. Immediately after the murder
Karl-Erik actually seems freed: "I felt a strange smile which
sat still in my face. Finally freed from the odor in me" (146).
But it is a form of liberation which implies psychic breakdown.
When Karl-Erik is taken away by the police he is screened
off from what he has done and is practically unreachable. The
murder of the child as an action by which Karl-Erik definitely
ridded himself of the child in him is in actuality spiritual suicide.

These two interpretations do not, however, exclude each
other. On the contrary, the complexity in the murder of the
child may well be an expression of the central antagonism in
Infantilia. Throughout the book Karl-Erik is torn between the
two different attitudes to life which Klem and Lucy represent,
and it is this tension which recurs in the final scene of the
novel. The murder of the child is primarily a last desperate
attempt at the alternative of surrender. But as an attempt
at finally eradicating the attraction to surrender, it is also a
last attempt at the alternative of living without love. The
murder of the child thereby demonstrates more clearly than
any other of Karl-Erik's actions how profoundly split he is.
Right up to the end he is incapable of rejecting one of the
women and trying wholeheartedly with the other. But with
the murder of the child, the contrast between Klem and Lucy
also appears painful and destructive. At the same time murder

and suicide, the death of the child signifies a doubly catastrophic result of Karl-Erik's attempt to orient himself in the field of tension between the alternative attitudes in *Infantilia.*

This very somber ending means that the trilogy comprised of Gyllensten's earliest books to a great extent terminated in an atmosphere of catastrophe and defeat. The heroic efforts to live without involvement and love from *Modern Myths* show themselves to be untenable, and endeavors to surrender to life in *The Blue Ship* turn out disastrously. Instead, the insight that human beings possess dangerous destructive and self-destructive impulses comes to the foreground in *Infantilia* in a more pronounced way than in the previous books. It is not easy to live, and in anger and disappointment we easily do violence to our fellow human beings. But almost more frightening is the realization that we can be so strongly attracted to our own annihilation and death. It would be exaggerating to say that the first period of Gyllensten's authorship resulted in a dead end. But it is as if the growing experience of the destructive forces in human beings upset the game for him and for a while led him to a much more pessimistic view of man's possibilities than in the previous books. It would take a long time before the light affirmation of life in *The Blue Ship* once again made its appearance in his writing.

IV *"Conversation Exercises"*

The view that the first period of Gyllensten's authorship ended in indomitable complications and insecurity about which way to proceed is further reinforced by the little book *Carnivora,* subtitled "Conversation exercises on a human voice level." It consists of more than sixty short prose pieces which deal with several different events of the times. The tone is satirical and ironic— often in an almost diabolical way. The priests in the Sacré-Coeur in Paris tell the tourists that the church remained unscathed by the bombing of World War II by a miracle. In *Carnivora,* with small and tricky means, the perspective is shifted: "God so loved Sacré-Coeur and its prelates that he let a large number of bombs and grenades fall on homes all around the world to demonstrate his mercy and love for his own more clearly" (53

cont.). But in spite of the often aggressive criticism there is
still a kind of resignation in *Carnivora*. Gyllensten lashes out
at the world's situation, but there are no cures in sight. Only
the heroic awareness, which refuses to conceal or smooth over
evil, can take a stand against the atrocities. Like *Infantilia*,
Carnivora is one if his darkest books.

Carnivora covers a large area. The rape of an eleven year
old girl leads a priest—who begets one child a year—to make
an inspired speech about the increasing brutality in the area
of sexuality. With all of his pompous words he has not the least
idea of the sexual distress behind the rape. A star surgeon
exploits sick people in testing new operating methods, and his
work is applauded in the newspapers while the patients die
in silence. A sports editor, who was attracted by Nazism in the
1930's, argues that youthful criminals ought naturally to get a
good old-fashioned Swedish whipping. A couple of pieces on
Toulouse-Lautrec stand apart: in spite of his drunkenness he
was a painter who saw with eyes wide-open. There are also
outbursts filled with empty pathos and anecdotes which are
almost bagatelles and ridiculous. To give an example: a general
who makes his bowel movement every morning in the presence
of his staff finally dies of diarrhea. These pieces appear as
species of linguistic grimaces which lead to confusion and
create a feeling of uncertainty about the seriousness of the book.

There are, however, two main themes running through the
book. One is an obstinate and well-executed criticism of Christianity. Gyllensten not only finds fault with narrow-minded priests
and remaining superstitions, but he attacks the Christian
faith itself. It ought to be mentioned that his attitude toward
Christianity is complex. There is evidence throughout his work
that he sees the Christian world of symbols as a meaningful
language, and in two pieces in *Carnivora* attempts at invalidat-
ing the Christian faith by finding it irreconcilable with logic
are discarded as childish.[6] But a moral repudiation of Christianity
is nevertheless dominant in *Carnivora*. Gyllensten sees tendencies to divide people into lambs and goats throughout the
whole of Christian history: the Christians are raised to the
heights thanks to the fact that the unfaithful are cast down into
eternal damnation. He cannot accept this mechanism, and it is

exposed with the same killing irony as in the piece on Sacré-Coeur. One piece is introduced with Jesus's words that the children may come to him and continues with the story of Herod's slaughter of all the baby boys in and around Bethlehem at the time of Jesus's birth. This massacre was in accord with the intentions of God, and it was also because of His arrangements that the Son and His family escaped all harm. In this way it was clear from the very beginning that Jesus was different from all others on earth. The following piece deals with one of the baby boys who ought to have been killed according to the command. But the soldier who was given the task was drunk, cut off his leg instead of his head and the boy survived as an invalid. As an adult it happened that he later met Jesus and Jesus offered to cure him. There, however, he thanked him proudly and said no: no one could give him back the thirty years he had lived as an invalid! *Carnivora* points out the terribly cruel side of Christianity and resolutely takes the victim's side.

The other main theme in *Carnivora* is a final coming to terms with Nazism. Gyllensten gives some glimpses of the brutality and sadism of the Nazis toward the Jews during the war years. He cannot get rid of the fear that Nazism remains under the surface and can break out again. But in most of the pieces, silence reigns after the great catastrophe. The little people have been killed by the war and cities lie in ruins. The moon rises in what was once Fischl's bedroom. The shadow of a dog urinating in Holert's living room is cast down two stories to the house next door and lands in the nettles in Büling's hall, and next spring the bird-cherry will bloom in the Hintze's kitchenette. For the shocked visitors from outside, innumerable bomb craters open up like yawning wells in the lawns. On the battlefield at Dunkirk the earth has been fertilized with blood and lymphatic fluids. A child picks wild strawberries growing there and in that way inherits the dead from the war. In the wine cellar *Zum roten Öchslein* a German group sings a noisy song:

> Wer soll das bezahlen,
> Wer hat das bestellt,
> Wer hat so viel Pinke-Pinke,
> Wer hat so viel Geld? (119)

(Who must pay,
Who has placed the order,
Who has that much dough,
Who has that much money?)

But it is glaringly obvious that nothing can pay for the millions
of people who were crippled and killed during the war.

The introductory piece of *Carnivora* is devoted to Goya, the
Spanish painter who described the cruelties of the Franco-Spanish
war in his etchings from the beginnings of the 1800's. Gyllensten
paints a suggestive picture of the painter who was deaf at that
time: an uninvited guest creeps around his silent house, his
name is Horror and the painter's hand knows how to recreate
human beings' pain and death. The last piece of the book, however, is signed Parrot and is a skeptical discussion of language.
The question is, what are words actually? And the answer is,
sounds which we can form all too easily in our mouths, an
inheritance with a high sentimental value, fragile traditions.
There is something nefarious in our ability to find words for
everything which makes words undependable. A verse about
love and dove makes us vibrate with emotions conditioned
by tradition. But there are also ironic verses about how a real
Aryan's heart rejoices every time a Jew is tortured in noisy pain.

In a new edition of *Carnivora* (1967) Gyllensten claimed
that it is between Goya and the Parrot that the book's pieces
take place. The Parrot is the fickle and vacuous chatterer who
glibly makes statements about everything between heaven and
earth. He has the word in those parts of the book which are
characterized by empty pathos, mockery, and obscenities. With
his presence Gyllensten wished to express his distrust for language and for the degree and durability of human convictions
and confessions in general. It is not only that the empty and
ridiculous words expose human beings as fools. The inflated outbursts also tend to lighten the weightiness of the serious positions. The voices heard in the book seem to melt together in a
meaningless and chaotic static. It is in this sense that the prose
pieces in *Carnivora* become conversational exercises on a
human voice level.

There is, however, no doubt that it is Goya's true insight and
emotion which dominates *Carnivora*. It may seem to be blas-

phemy to link Christianity with Nazism and is in many respects unjust. But in *Carnivora* both Nazism and Christianity are presented as dogmas in whose name the faithful persecuted and murdered other people in appalling numbers. A few times the perspective is expanded to include all of the West's politics of expansion: "But it was given to the West to conquer the earth, to spread the white man throughout the world, shoot and control, sell and tame, buy and bend" (60 cont.). For Gyllensten, as for Goya, the world is a battlefield, where people inflict all conceivable and inconceivable torments upon each other. As in *Modern Myths,* irony functions as a means of defense against overwhelming reality. But at the base of *Carnivora* is an almost wordless horror in the face of the cruelties of the world and a furious but impotent protest. It is probably the impotence which makes the horror so very keen.

Perhaps Goya and the Parrot are basically so incompatible that *Carnivora* is almost split into two books: sometimes one reads it like a grotesque choir of clamoring voices, sometimes like a genuine and violent protest. But it is thanks to this ambiguity that *Carnivora* established in a remarkable way two of the most central motifs in the first period of Gyllensten's authorship. On the one hand is the experience of the world as an absurd arrangement without goal or meaning where high and low and tragic and ridiculous are mixed together in an outrageous way. On the other hand there is the almost inconceivably abundant suffering in the world which is real enough and which stirs up his anger. The tension between these two "visions" returns in his continuing production, but he attacks the problem from somewhat different points of departure.

CHAPTER 3

Distance Toward Life

Carnivora was published in 1953, and it was not until 1956 that Gyllensten returned to the scene with the novel *Senilia*. As far as one can see, the process of reorientation after *Infantilia* seems to have been both long and profound. The year before *Senilia* came out, however, Gyllensten published an essay by the same name in which he discussed the problem of the form of the novel: "Senilia. Reflections on Narration and on Thomas Mann." He juxtaposed two of the most noted novelists of the 1900's: James Joyce and Thomas Mann. The point of departure is a comparison which Mann made between himself and Joyce on a few pages in *The Story of a Novel*. Mann had just read Harry Levin's book on Joyce and felt he had discovered several unexpected similarities between himself and Joyce— especially the fact that they both described the downfall of the middle-class. But according to Gyllensten, it seems as if Mann feared that his novels gave the impression of bland traditionalism next to Joyce's position in the eccentric avant-garde.

Gyllensten clearly takes Mann's part in this comparison. To a certain extent at least he seems to view Joyce as a representative of a form of realism which implies that the author steps out of his work and pretends to render reality as if he himself did not exist. But this type of realism is incompatible with Gyllensten's epistemological and aesthetic positions; for him, every description of reality includes a subject with a definite set of values and way of looking at things; and thus in every novel there is, finally, a novelist speaking. Thus a novelist's ambition to be invisible is actually only a special and suggestive technique he uses to communicate indirectly with his readers and it can be compared to an occult seance. In Mann, however, Gyllensten finds an open recognition of the author's presence in the novel which is honest and which retains the basic epic assumption that someone narrates something for someone else. In this way it is not a question of naive novel writing for Mann, but of a form of legends: "a narrator's work with the narrator immanent in the work."[1] Gyllensten's final judgment is that Mann, through this deliberate distance to fiction, is in an avant-garde position similar to Joyce's.

Gyllensten's preference for Mann's position was not, however, totally impersonal. It is obvious that his description of Mann's narrative art was also a declaration of his own narrative intentions in the novels which were to come. There is no doubt that he modelled the novels which comprise his second period with Mann as his example. In the first place he abandoned the first-person narrator of the first period in favor of the third person. But even more important is the fact that he, like Mann, gave the narrator such a prominent role in the novel: the task of the narrator is not only to relate the action, but also to make extensive comments on that which takes place through learned reflections and profound analyses. Much of Mann's almost ceremoniously rich language recurs in the language Gyllensten himself developed. Furthermore, Gyllensten also took up Mann's ironic narrative tone, which accentuates the narrator's presence in the work often in a playful way. One can hardly over-emphasize the extent to which this narrative method lies in line with the aesthetic positions Gyllensten adopted early, and Mann's novel-writing must therefore have struck him as something of a revelation. Finally, Gyllensten also seems to have directly taken over another technique from Mann which further reinforces the presence of the narrator. He writes that the Joseph-series is like a monologue:

... it is a narrative, not a polyphonic configuration, an old man speaks for himself—the same voice, the same learned spirituality and playful-ceremonious entanglement speaks from the mouth of little Benjamen as from old Jacob's, from Mut-em-enet's as from Joseph's, from the child's, the old man's, the woman's, and the man's.[2]

In a similar way, all of the people in Gyllensten's novels from the second period speak practically the same language as the

narrator and the effect is that one hears the narrator's voice
through the voices of the novel's characters. The narrator's voice
is always clearly audible as in Mann's novels.

Gyllensten's connection with Mann was naturally not only
formal in character. For Mann the ironic narrative primarily
serves a critical purpose: he throws light on the characters in
his novels, lifts up their secret motivations and reveals their
idiosyncrasies and follies. Similarly, Gyllensten's ironic narrative
method is at its core critical. Narration in the third person
meant that he could keep his figures at a completely different
distance than in his earlier books, and the ironic narrative
comment presented even more possibilities for critical illumination. The people the narrator describes are important, but the
critical perspective the narrator establishes in relation to them
is just as important. The novels take on a structure which is
reminiscent of didactic novels: the heroes of the novel grope
in the dark, but the narrator has all the answers. The narrator
is often presented as a good and eager pedagogue, who rejects
dangerous ambitions and hostile instincts. Therefore, in his novels
from the second period Gyllensten in many ways follows the
skeptical line from *Modern Myths*. He rejects a set of destructive
convictions and defends the simple life of everyday.

I *Turning Oneself into an Old Man*

Senilia was a great venture on Gyllensten's part, and it also
became one of his most remarkable novels. Furthermore, it is
one of his broadest novels in scope. On the autumn day in
1955 in which the action takes place nothing much happens—
at least not on the surface. Thirty-eight-year-old Torsten Lerr
struggles to wake up, then eats breakfast with Ester—much
younger than he and with whom he lives—reads aloud for her
so that she can practice her stenography, and finally goes out
for a walk with the dog. But during the hours covered by the
action he goes through large areas of his life in his memory
and all of these memories comprise the history of a whole
family. As the fate of Torsten's family is unrolled it also becomes
clear that *Senilia* is closely related to *Infantilia*—something already suggested by the titles. The most obvious link between

the two books lies in the fact that Karl-Erik once again reappears as a character, this time called Gunnar Gren. But in
a broader sense there is, throughout *Senilia*, a fierce polemic
against the mentality Karl-Erik represents. *Senilia* thus is a
very conscious effort to come to terms with the catastrophic
complications which were the results of *Infantilia*.

Torsten's memories are not rendered in chronological order,
and the same episodes recur in several places in the book. He
spins several threads. But the different events glide into each
other and finally build a coherent weave. The family history
begins with Torsten's father.[3] Hemming Lerr, an engineer,
amassed a fortune during many years abroad and at about the
age of sixty moved to live in a large house in the small town
of Eksjö in southern Sweden. At this point Torsten was just
born, but his mother never came to Sweden. It is probable
that she died in Torsten's childbirth, but it is also possible that
she left his father—here, as on several other important points,
it is impossible for Torsten to reach absolute certainty, and
instead he must try to fit the puzzle together with several different
possible interpretations. That his father was involved in an
accidental explosion and became blind was, however, terrifyingly
clear. Torsten was ten years old at the time and his father's
blindness left a great mark upon his childhood. His feelings
for his father became complex. On the one hand he was close
to him and felt sympathy with his deterioration before his death:
the trembling hands, the increasing obesity, food stains on his
shirt and trousers. He remembers that his father continued to
play classical music on the piano, but that as he forgot the
notes the melodies became more and more fragmentary. In
general, the father was surrounded by an increasing desolation.
On the other hand, his father's blindness became a burden to
him. His father forced him to read aloud to him several hours
every day and as the years went by Torsten came to hate these
reading periods. Along with sympathy he began to feel anger
at his father's excessive interference in his life, but his father
was struck by misfortune and thus it was impossible to give
free rein to his anger. Thus a painful feeling of guilt runs
throughout Torsten's memories of his father.

Torsten's relations to the women of the family are no less

complicated. Instead of his mother, Gunhild came to keep house in the large villa with the old man and the child. But she also became his father's mistress. Once as a child Torsten discovered a secret passage in the closets between their bedrooms and the discovery set off his developing sexuality. Gunhild became desirable to him and he became his father's rival. Judging from appearances it seems as though his father sent Gunhild to him a few years later to initiate him into the mysteries of sex, but he ran away from her then. However, Gunhild became his mistress after his father's death, and they obviously had a good relationship. It was she who awakened Torsten's lust, and his desire for her continued to burn intensely in him. Torsten cherishes her with more warmth than anyone else in the family, and the memory of her red hair still makes him miss her intensely. Perhaps it is also partly because of Gunhild that he now lives together with Ester. Ester is Gunhild's daughter and also possibly Torsten's father's child—Torsten speaks a little jokingly about his "Egyptian relationships" (43). But she could also be the daughter of a major to whom Gunhild was married a few years immediately after his father's death. In any case it is clear that Ester stirs Torsten's desire in the same bold and trembling way that Gunhild did. She moves him in a way no other woman has since Gunhild, and this leaves him at the mercy of her favors.

The fates of both Gunhild and Ester are interwoven with Gunnar Gren, who was Torsten's childhood playmate. With a technique which would become characteristic of his novel-writing, Gyllensten has given Gunnar traits from one of his earlier characters. As the different names imply, Gunnar is not identical with Karl-Erik in *Infantilia*, and above all his background is different. Gunnar grew up in a teacher's home in a thick atmosphere of voluptuous and guilt-ridden sexuality. Torsten once showed Gunnar the family's serving girl. Her name was Elsa, she was buxom and used to shower in the basement without closing the curtain. In extreme excitement Gunnar crawled closer to the window on all fours and in Torsten's eyes he behaved like a rutting dog. But Gunnar's relationship with Karl-Erik is nonetheless clear: he has committed almost exactly the same child murder as Karl-Erik.

Once, when Torsten was away, he looked up Ester and forced himself upon her with his lewd love. Ester had then a new-born child, and like Karl-Erik he became jealous and took the child into the bathroom to drown it. He regretted it at the last minute and let himself slip on the wet floor instead. The baby landed in the sink, uninjured, but Ester later sent it away to relatives. Gunnar, however, cracked his skull, spent a long time in the hospital and later was repeatedly treated in a mental hospital. The same destructive pattern is repeated in Gunnar's relationship to Gunhild and Elsa. Although married to Elsa, Gunnar also forced himself on the aging Gunhild and created difficult conflicts between the two women. One, according to Torsten, "many times cursed and detested and not as yet really surmounted sacrificial day" they took each other's life in what apparently was an automobile accident (16 cont.). It is not only a question of a confusing family history. The ironic narrative tone cannot hide the fact that Torsten has gone through very difficult and painful experiences.

The whole of this family history is once again actualized in *Senilia*. On the present level Gunnar once again seeks contact with Ester, and it is obvious that she does not completely reject him. Torsten well understands what is happening—though not in detail. In spite of Gunnar's clumsy attempts to disguise his voice he recognized it on the telephone. He thinks he notices a different smell behind Ester's ear, and perhaps she and Gunnar have already met. In any case, he thinks he knows that Gunnar has invited Ester out to a restaurant this evening. In other words, Torsten and Gunnar are once again in a relationship of rivalry to each other. Previously they had been rivals first for Gunhild and later for Ester. Now they are once again rivals for Ester, and all three are thus placed in a highly charged situation.

The basic tension of *Senilia* lies in the conflict between Torsten and Gunnar. Torsten and Gunnar are not only rivals for the same woman, they also represent two very different attitudes toward life which are strongly opposed to each other in the novel and which can be concretized in the pair of opposites "old man"–"child." In *Senilia* the child is given somewhat different characteristics than those given in the analysis of *Infantilia*, and everything regarded as childish receives both a stronger and a more clearly negative charge. This shift in the evaluation of childishness is also accentuated by a development in terminology. In *Infantilia,* the child's ability to surrender itself is largely presented as something positive and worth striving for. But in *Senilia* this surrender is described as a lack of distance to life, and this lack of distance appears as the child's most characteristic trait. Although in body an old man, Gunhild's father lived like a child, according to Torsten, and some of the good childishness remained in him. He had no concept of time, and life for him was "a blessed state": "...an eager and childish gliding between incomparable and immeasurable states, eternities, of longing, boredom, despair, happiness, hope and continuous, enjoyable changes, seductions and surrenders" (15).

But in *Senilia* the child above all others is Gunnar; and he too is without distance to his feelings, experiences, and actions. For his part, however, the lack of distance is dangerous in a completely different way. As opposed to Gunhild's peaceful father, he is not filled primarily with good and pleasurable feelings. Instead he is ridden by a manifold of other emotional states which are characterized as childish in the novel: fear, jealousy, despair. Without the ability to keep his distance from these emotions, he is in actuality a slave to them. He is not capable either of directing his actions or of taking responsibility for them. Using one of Torsten's many invectives he "glues" himself to other people with his shameful needs and confused demands. His childishness lies not least in the fact that he turns to others for the satisfaction of his needs, and in practice this means that he tries to live like a parasite. "Take care of me! Take care of me! I am so lonely!" is his plea to them (74). This lack of distance becomes devastating when his childish feelings and demands become destructive. Since he cannot create distance to the situations in which he lands, it is impossible for him to resist and conquer his impulses to hurt himself and others. Instead, all of the aggressiveness and despair within him are allowed free rein.

In conscious and explicit contrast to Gunnar, Torsten forms and practices an old man's attitude toward life, the most distinctive feature of which is just distance to life. In this way

Torsten is a sharp and obstinate critic of Gunnar's attitude throughout the novel, and behind him the novel's narrator advocates the same critical perspective. In this manner Torsten to a certain extent builds upon ideas his father has given him; and in spite of the complications between them, his father stands as a kind of model for him. "The old man" in *Senilia* is Torsten's father, but it is also Torsten himself who, in his father's footsteps, attempts to arrive at an old man's attitude. Using another term from the father, the old man's distance to life implies that one "detaches oneself" from oneself and one's surroundings. According to Torsten's ideas, this detachment presupposes a mature person's familiarity with life and its situations. Torsten has the first volume of *Joseph and His Brothers* on his bedside table (48), and, like Mann throughout the whole of the Joseph series, he believes that life repeats itself to a great extent. Only one who is capable of recognizing the events and conflicts he meets as something already well-known has distance to himself and life, according to Torsten. Therefore he wishes to become familiar with his life by telling the story of it to himself. Here is one of the passages in which he formulates what he calls his "program" most clearly:

It was a question of stretching out one's life so ambitiously, of telling oneself into every inch and every whim and on every occasion, which occurred to him, so that in the end it became clear to his very nature that he recognized it and could not let himself be terrified or transformed. (73)

This process implies going backward in time (cf. Kierkegaard!) and narrating one's memories. But at the same time the narration is aimed toward the present: it is through a familiarity with the past that it is possible to recognize oneself in present events. With the formula that Torsten inherited from his father, narration creates the ability to lay "the cane of familiarity" over the present and the future. As opposed to the child who finds himself in the midst of the tumult of existence, Torsten attempts to meet the present with the distance alloted by familiarity.

Several times Torsten is given the opportunity to state his

program even more precisely. In the beginning of the novel he develops what he calls a dogma of corporeality in connection with Plotinus the philosopher. In a mocking way which takes the edge off his seriousness he claims that the body is "the organ for our surprises, the play-room and play-ground for coincidences, the sphere of the senses where changes and terrors crowd each other for light." Here the body is the "forum of childishness." But the body is also as old "as a trait of the species or a family name, old as the street where our forefathers walked and tramped" (38). Thus what happens within the body can still be recognized, given a name, and narrated. But the memory and the narration are the old man's. The relationship between the body and narration can therefore be seen as a tension between the child and the old man and in this sense there is something of the child and the old man in every person. What is old-mannish in Torsten's program is the fact that he rejects his body and instead places narration on the throne. With a firm hand he lays "the cane of familiarity" upon the child within him. One must say that his attitude toward life implies an extreme intellectualization of existence.

Of all the things which come to him through his body, Torsten is especially on his guard against emotions. His skepticism of all forms of affected sensitivity is profound: "Torsten was thoroughly tired of all sensitivity—the crying, sighing, languishing, hiccuping, sanctimonious game of vanity" (119). Early in the novel he violently rejects people who cannot live unless they are in the grip of strong emotions. They cultivate their emotions and are in despair when their feelings fail them. He links this way of living to Christianity's fear of the alien and death and also characterizes it as "the faith of a child" (26). Torsten rejects all of this childish sentimentality in favor of what he refers to as "Greek pride," which does not need to be constantly conquered by emotions. He places the sober paganism of "Goethe's marble Greeks" (26) in contrast to these feverish emotions. Torsten's rejection of Christ further on in the novel is a counterpart to this comment. Instead Torsten feels sympathy for Ahasueros, "the man of resistance and the heathen." Here again Christianity is seen as "the child's pathetic politics," the goal of which is to preserve human beings beyond death (142).

But he especially rejects the pretense that love can be preserved so that it will last throughout life. He himself finds love much less constant and cannot forgive Jesus the fact that Judas was sacrificed "as fuel in the pedagogics of love" (143). Instead he strives to keep a reasonable distance to love and its demands:

He who is indifferent is loveless in that he fails in love's preposterous deeds and absurd claims and thus draws upon him the lover's disdain and curse. But he is also merciful in that he at the same time fails in love's sacrificial deeds and cruel rites of initiation and refrains from hate's and fear's terrifying transformations of the loved one. (144)

Torsten places the old man's coolness and indifference in contrast to sentimental love and in this respect too his program implies the old man's punishment of the child.

In the light of Torsten's reasoning and position, the events of the present receive their full implications. During the hours encompassed in the novel he is completely occupied with the practice of his program. When he wakes up in the morning he has an erection and is certainly no old man, but his ceremonious and droning monologue is an exercise in the old man's attitude he advocates and thus even linguistically *Senilia* becomes an antithesis to *Infantilia*. It is not only that the events of the present awaken Torsten's past to life in an often very sensual way—here Gyllensten has certainly learned from Proust[4]—but Torsten also goes through his memories voluntarily and very consciously in order to, in the words of the program, "tell oneself into every inch and every whim." It is certainly the reawakened rivalry with Gunnar which actualizes the conflicts in Torsten's earlier life, but the whole memory process is still directed toward the present: by carefully going through his experiences Torsten wishes to recognize and make himself familiar with the situation Gunnar's appearance implies. With an old man's recognition and distance he strives to meet the former rival's reappearance and the difficult situation in which he and Ester are placed.

As Örjan Lindberger has pointed out, the goal of this training in "old-mannishness" is to a great extent the disarmament of pain.[5] The experiences Torsten has behind him have been very painful, and it still hurts to remember them. However, by placing himself at a distance to his experiences he can take the edge off the pain they awaken. This process becomes especially clear in his use of the popular music which is heard through the ceiling from his neighbor above. By using the songs as ironic comments on his memories he gets perspective on his feelings and prevents them from overwhelming him. The irony functions throughout *Senilia* in this way, as a defense against things which are too painful. But it may also be that Torsten's training is meant even more to disarm the dangerous and destructive impulses which the rivalry with Gunnar awakens in him. There is no doubt that the high tension which lies under the everyday events of the present is generated by the fact that Torsten has a strong attack of jealousy, and this jealousy runs throughout the whole of the novel: it is already there in his morning dream, moves down in a song about a cuckold from the neighbor above, and prowls around a book Ester has probably received as a present from Gunnar. His reactions to the song especially reveal his trouble in keeping his jealousy at a distance and also reveal its depth. First he believes he hears the strained scorn of the cuckold, then sees it as a recognition of the power of jealousy and in turn ridicules the song. Later he understands that in reality he is scorning the strained superiority he assumes in relation to his jealousy. He cannot escape from the grip of jealousy.

Seen against the background of Torsten's family history it is not difficult to understand why it is so important for him to keep his jealousy at a distance. Jealousy is also the central theme in the memories he calls forth, and it stands out as something very destructive. The many love triangles which are described are all darkly and forebodingly charged, and several of them lead directly to catastrophe. In Gunnar's case jealousy results in the murderous attempt on Ester's child and his own self-mutilation, and behind Gunhild's and Elsa's automobile accident lies their rivalry for Gunnar. In the light of these devastating actions Torsten's training in old-mannishness must primarily be seen as a conscientious attempt at disarming the destructive force of jealousy. There is a jealous child inside who is complaining loudly and making difficulties—as Torsten himself admits several times, he is not at all so far away from Gunnar as he would like to have it appear. But his training means that he is working to put his jealousy at a distance. By narrating his memories he can recognize his own jealousy, once again see how dangerous it is, and dissociate himself from it. Thanks to the fact that he can keep himself at a distance from his jealousy he can consider its consequences when faced with it and keep it under control.

On the last page of *Senilia* Gunnar throws stones at Ester's window, and in order to leave them alone in peace with each other Torsten gets up to go out with the dog. This is Torsten's only meaningful action in the present and it also stands out as something very significant. As Lindberger has demonstrated, everything in the novel which has to do with dogs and doggishness is associated with both "rutting" and with "fidelity."[6] The dog which in the present wags its tail around Torsten's and Ester's feet is called Fidelio and symbolizes the fidelity in love in which Torsten does not believe. When Torsten goes out with the dog and leaves Gunnar and Ester free it means that he rejects the childish demands he still has somewhere that Ester should be faithful to him. But in several other episodes in *Senilia* the aspect of rutting is emphasized—for example when Gunnar crawls like a rutting dog in front of Elsa in the shower. As in *Infantilia*, the dog symbolism expresses a complex experience of sexuality: an excitement which is not only of desire but which also includes rancor and is therefore destructive in character. In the final chapter of *Senilia*, when Torsten thinks that his shadow lies "greedily glued to the floor like a dog afraid of being hit" (265) around Ester's feet, some of this "ruttishness" appears again: because of jealousy his love for Ester has assumed a destructive character. Thus his action of going out with the dog also means that he reins in his jealousy, and as such it stands out as the result of his arduous training. He rejects his jealousy, in contrast to Gunnar, and refuses to give it free rein. By going out he definitely casts off jealousy and the actions and entanglements in which it could involve him. Torsten is afraid that Ester will be hurt in the charged situation which has arisen thanks to Gunnar's return, but he does not feel he can do anything without making it even more dangerous. With deliberateness and at a distance he therefore lets the affair between them run its course. It is not without effort that he leaves Ester: "brusquely" he offers to go out with the dog (272). But it is just thanks to this that Torsten's exit becomes a clear and definite manifestation of the reflective distance to the present and its events which is, according to his comments, the distinguishing trait of an old man's attitude to life.

Still, one cannot say that *Senilia* presents an absolutely complete solution—the perspectives of Torsten and the narrator do not totally coincide. There is an element of uncertainty and complication in Torsten's final exit which can be referred back to an ambiguity inherent in the old-mannish attitude. Does Torsten's exit perhaps mean that he goes out in loneliness and isolation? A similar transition is to be found in the presentation of the old-mannish attitude: familiarity and distance are also described as boredom and emptiness. Sometimes the attitude to the child and to childishness is also ambiguous. Using the formula Torsten has inherited from his father, his training in old-mannishness implies that he lays the "cane of familiarity" on the child within him. From this point of view his training can be characterized as a process of maturity and the old man's attitude toward life as maturity. But a cane is a tool of punishment used against the child and thus at the same time the formula suggests that perhaps an act of violence is also committed against the child in this process. With these ambiguities *Senilia* anticipates the novel *Juvenilia*, and thus *Infantilia, Senilia* and *Juvenilia* compose a trilogy of ages in Gyllensten's work.

Still there is no doubt that Gyllensten presented Torsten's program as his own strategy, and it is clear that it plays a central part in the second period of his authorship. The program is very personally constructed and it is hardly possible simply to refer it back to any of the historical philosophies of life. In view of the many references to classical philosophical thinking in *Senilia*, one could perhaps characterize it as a type of stoic attitude. To begin with, the aim of the program is to retain one's calm and reason in difficult and complicated situations. Furthermore, one's own passions are to be exposed and conquered. The insight that certain forces in human beings are dangerous and destructive is necessary and unavoidable. And finally, possibilities for action are regarded with a great degree of skepticism. The situation seems so difficult that new attempts at action only seem to make things worse; therefore for the time being there is nothing better to do than lie low. It is certainly not a question of any hope that things will soon be better, but of enduring difficult misfortune stoically. Seen thus, the program is not only a great attempt at surmounting the complications so acutely presented in *Infantilia*; all of these components are also central themes in the other novels of the second period. Torsten's program would be carried on by the ironic narrator in *The Senator* and *The Death of Socrates*.

II *A Confused Social Reformer*

Discussing Thomas Mann in the essay entitled "Senilia," Gyllensten made the distinction between two kinds of novels: those which are monologues and those which are dialogues.[7] The novel *Senilia* is clearly a monologue: the perspective is always Torsten's and the narrator stands close behind him as his prompter. *The Senator* is, however, much more a dialogue, though this structure does not mean that Gyllensten has abandoned his ironic narrative position. In *The Senator*, the narrator stands at a distance to all of his figures. The novel has a protagonist, to be sure, who is always in the center: Antonin Bhör, a middle-aged senator who lives in an unnamed communistic country and who has lost his faith in the social revolution he himself helped to drive through. But the novel consists of a series of confrontations between Senator Bhör and a line of other characters. A young boy, an unusual woman, and the senator's boss each in turn direct sharp and penetrating criticism toward him. The main purpose of the novel is this critical illumination of Senator Bhör and the criticism is formulated primarily via these confrontations.

The Senator begins, however, with a suggestive scene which functions as an introduction to the story of the confused senator. In the first chapter of the novel Bhör is the chairman of a judicial committee which has just completed a difficult case. It seems that a retarded woman has accused two male boarders of sexual aggression, but the committee has not been able to produce any evidence with which to sentence the men. Thus, although Bhör and the other members of the committee realize that her story is true, the case is dismissed. Bhör has an attack of a recurring fever, and the situation appears before him with intrusive sharpness. Standing by the committee-room window he sees the two brutal men force themselves and the submissive woman through the door to her home, and after a while the curtain behind her window is drawn and he thinks he hears a weak peeping, as from a mouse: the sado-masochistic game between the men and the woman continues. It is quiet in the meeting room and Bhör feels the committee members' sympathy for the woman and their pangs of conscience. But the case has also awakened a "heavy and ruthless lust" in them. Bhör feels that they have exposed "needs directed towards disintegration and destruction" (10) for each other. The scene presents an explanation for the senator's ideological doubts. Justice does not function in the new society he has helped to build up either, people do violence to each other as usual. But it also reveals a destructiveness which flows like a dark current throughout the whole of *The Senator*. "In intoxication and fever, there lie our passions and our desire," Bhör states bitterly (8).

Thus Bhör's fever is not only a physiological phenomenon. Perhaps he has even helped in the emergence of the illness. In any case it is clear that he uses the fever as a cover for his ideological crisis. Under cover of the fever he dares to think rebellious and forbidden thoughts, and it gives him an alibi for staying away from his work. Bhör's sharp-eyed boss guesses at the connection and orders him to travel to a health spa for two weeks. During this trip Bhör plunges deeper and deeper into his crisis: when he lets go of his self-discipline he is plunged into profound despair. During this trip he meets the boy and the woman. His meeting with the young boy takes place in the elevator of the senator's hotel. He drops his newspaper, the boy picks it up for him, and there is a strong and unsettling contact between them. First Bhör suspects that it is just a question of a homosexual invitation from the boy, but later he remembers that the boy must be the younger brother of a rebellious leader he had helped to sentence to a long term in prison. He wonders if the boy wants to take revenge on him now, but at the same time he feels strongly identified with him. He looks him up again, tells him about his own youth and in this way reveals the background for his crisis. It becomes clear that Bhör grew up under very difficult circumstances before the revolution. His mother was forced to move into one of the larger cities in order to support herself. There she worked in an unhealthy laundry and was shoved together with about a dozen other people in a little room with a bucket in the corner for a toilet at night. She soon contracted tuberculosis and died at the age of only twenty-six. Bhör only really understood her fate when he read about the English child-laborers several years later in the first book of *Das Kapital*. For the first time in his life he felt that someone really sought him out, wanted to force and influence him and therefore pleaded to him nakedly, boldy, and ruthlessly.

This meeting with Marx was decisive for Bhör. He felt included in a fellowship which cared about him and which made demands on him. He felt almost physically that he was a part of a common body along with his social kindred spirits, and he saw something divine in the historical process. He became a socialist the way others believe in God, and on the basis of this vision he dedicated his life to the revolution and to the work of rebuilding society. Seen against the background of his youthful devotion, his crisis becomes comprehensible. By losing his faith in socialism he also loses the vital and intimate fellowship he experienced with the people around him. Instead of finding a meaning in social developments he now feels he hears only "guttural groans and bubbling without address" around him (76). No one seeks him any longer: he is abandoned to himself, and the situation fills him with anxiety and despair. The boy has remained silent during Bhör's long and passionate monologue, but finally he replies in an unexpected way: with a sentimental song about a little child who gets lost in the cold winter, he ridicules the senator's confession. It is obvious that he finds Bhör unendurably pathetic, and he leaves him with an obscene gesture.

The senator's second meeting also begins dramatically. After his confrontation with the boy he sits in a garden and looks back on his life as a politician. He and the other leaders drew

up plans for a land of happiness without classes, force, or op-
pression. But now he thinks that he really helped to create
a new hierarchy of commanders and subordinates with even
more force than before. "The Tower of Babel! The Tower of
Babel" (104)—this is a recurring symbol in the novel for how
their attempts have resulted in their opposites. Bhör's bitterness
is so great that he grinds his teeth without noticing it, and in
this mood he goes to one of the windows of the restaurant and
a woman catches sight of him from inside. It turns out that
her name is Elisa, and later she tells him that she was fascinated
by the sight of him. First she was frightened by the ghostly
lit face on the other side of the window pane. But then she
thought she saw a truly naked human being: fear, desire, and
passion were in his eyes and it was as if he sucked on her with
those eyes. After this intense eye contact Elisa leaves her group
for the senator's sake; they drive away in her car and spend
two days together in an out of the way inn in the country.
Gyllensten gave *The Senator* a subtitle, "A Melodrama," and it is
apparent that he uses melodramatic effects in a playful way.

The time Elisa and the senator spend together comprises an
undulating dialectic: sometimes they are strongly opposed to
each other with incompatible points of view, and sometimes
they think almost the same thoughts; sometimes they find that
they have significant similarities, and other times they realize
that their search leads them in opposite directions. In the beginning the senator meets Elisa in the same straightforward way as
the boy. When they leave the restaurant together the senator
attempts to take her arm, but she hisses at him not to behave
like a schoolboy—this is no infatuation! Later on in the car she
mockingly answers his speech about how it feels to be in the
grasp of a great task: "Tra—la! So declamatory! Can't you take
off your political preaching cape, Mr. Social-Builder!" (119).
She possesses a sober and completely unsentimental passion
which is in sharp contrast to Bhör's pathetic rhetoric. Can't one
use oneself with benevolent skepticism and a suitable amount
of indifference, she asks him.

As they come closer to each other, however, the deeper
points of contact between them come clearer. During one of
their long conversations, Elisa thoughtfully calls herself Pasiphae.

Bhör does not really understand what she is referring to, but the narrator retells and interprets the classic myth and uses it to characterize Elisa. According to the narrator, Pasiphae had experienced a love of princely measure together with the king of Crete. But like everything else human, this love was not perfect and she desired something completely different and superhuman. The bull to whom she gave herself could surely be thought to be below the lowest of humans, but actually was a god. Therefore Pasiphae's longing must not be seen as an attraction to the bestial. On the contrary, what she sought was superhuman in the sense that it was stronger and more whole than weak human beings. In the narrator's interpretation the inhuman is divine in character, and there is no doubt that his words are valid for Elisa as well.

Retold in this way, the myth reveals both the similarities and the differences between Elisa and the senator. As they both state, they feel poor and unsatisfied with only themselves to turn to. They seek something else: "We are searching for something greater than we are. We seek something more powerful than ourselves" (159). But while Bhör wishes to find human traits and marks of recognition in the world around him, this is Elisa's wish:

Graft onto me! Grant unto me! There is only one prayer, if there ever were any prayers—the prayer of all women: break through my boundaries and place an ungovernable stranger in my center! Give me to something which is not me! (128)

As opposed to Bhör, she is not seeking another person as her image and equal, but like Pasiphae she wishes to be struck by something totally different. True passion has no human face, she declares. In the end she attempts to arrive at a reality which lies beyond all human weaknesses and limitations and in this way she foreshadows a theme which Gyllensten would develop further in *Cain's Memoirs* and *Juvenilia*.

Elisa is such a fascinating character that she overshadows Bhör for a while, but within the framework of *The Senator* her derisive and sarcastic criticism is nevertheless the most important thing. According to her the senator is actually only a naive and

power-hungry egocentric, who bears in himself what she calls the
quintessence of the Christian burden. Christianity taught that
the human being stands in the center of creation and that teaching has also been the basis for the senator's political striving.
But he has not succeeded because the world is not a home
for the human being: the world is not made for people, and
it does not adjust itself to them. This fact is neither tragic nor
precarious, it is just the way things are. She frankly declares
to the senator; "It is much more terrifying and much more
fantastic to live than you and your equals deserve!" (149).
Bhör has primarily appreciated the tenderness which has existed
between them during the days they spent together, but when
they leave each other the contrast between them becomes
obvious: while she roars away in her powerful car he remains
standing on the dusty street full of childish feelings of
abandonment.

   Certain elements of the thriller are included in the melodramatic effects in *The Senator*. During Bhör's stay at the health
spa his boss telephones him several times to check his where-
abouts and when he returns home a policeman awaits him with
a drawn pistol. The thriller-like atmosphere of *The Senator*
culminates in Bhör's final visit to his boss. Late at night the
senator is driven to a well-guarded palace, and the governor
acts out a threatening comedy for him. He has just thrown away
a flower which has been bold enough to leave a spot on his
suit jacket, and he implies in insinuating words that Bhör can
receive the same treatment if he continues to make trouble. The
meeting ends without the reader's knowledge of the senator's
final fate, but beforehand the sharp old man delivers a series
of critical comments which are in accord with the boy's and
Elisa's criticism. First he urges Bhör with relatively good humor
to take it easy with the human aspects—after all, nothing can
cost more than one's life! But he later sharpens his tone and
accuses the senator of bringing forth gods and archangels so
that the whole universe reverberates with his private life: "An-
noyances and trifles? No, we can't have that, good heavens—you
want thunder and lightning, sin, guilt, mercy, and the whole
bit in the wind-harp!" (238). In his heart and soul, he concludes,
the senator is nothing but a reactionary individualist, who tries

to enlighten the world with his prejudices and then is afraid of the dark when he does not know where he is. This is a final judgment which implies a complete rejection of the senator's experiences; and in contrast to him, the governor himself stands for an almost brutal objectivity both in political deeds and in his private life.

There is a well-known literary work which can aid in illuminating the meaning of the story of Senator Bhör. With the intensive contact between the middle-aged senator and the young boy, Gyllensten has given a reference to Thomas Mann's *Death in Venice*. Bhör's immediate and strong attraction to the boy, the boy's beauty and the atmosphere of sensuality surrounding him and the pervading erotic tone between them—all of this turns the episode with the boy into something of a paraphrase of Gustav von Aschenbach's infatuation with the handsome Polish boy he meets in the Lido. And there is, perhaps, another reflection of Mann's short novel in *The Senator*. Toward the end of the novel von Aschenbach attempts to leave Venice in order to break the spell he is under, but he comes too late to the train and happily returns. In the same way the senator lets a plane fly from him on one occasion because he does not really wish to return home (44). But more important than these concrete similarities is the fact that the ambiguity which is so characteristic of *Death in Venice* has its counterpart in *The Senator*. Von Aschenbach's infatuation is an adoration of beauty Platonic in character, but at the same time the Polish boy is sensually very present. In a corresponding way the senator tells himself that he only wishes to tell the boy about himself, but the body and voice of the boy still force themselves close to him.

However, the points of contact between the two novels are not only limited to the episode with the boy. In general, *Death in Venice* points to the actual core of *The Senator*. Von Aschenbach's infatuation has a somber basis in reality. He has been a tense German idealist, who has met life with moral decisiveness and control. But his personality has become more and more impoverished with time and there is a strong death wish in his adoration of beauty. *Death in Venice* is therefore not only about an almost transcendental beauty, but also about a human being moving toward his downfall and disintegra-

tion. In a similar way Senator Bhör's political deeds have slipped
out of his grasp, the force which motivated him has left him,
and in his despair an attraction to death is conceived. Bhör is
very aware of this himself and constructs a whole philosophy
of death. He tells himself that death is something which everyone
has in common and a place where people must come together.
With an almost sensuous fascination he sees death as a funnel
through which humanity is finally pressed and he is attracted
to this destruction. A recurrent situation runs as a *leit-motif*
throughout the novel: the senator stands next to a window and
feels drawn to the depths below him. When everything else
has deserted him he still feels called to death as to a ceremonious
meeting. This feeling culminates when he is called to the
governor's palace: he thinks he will finally be nailed to something which is greater than he is. But the governor only wants
to check his dependability, and their meeting throws him into
even deeper confusion. He cannot find the irrevocable reality
he seeks so desperately even in death.

The Senator is a novel with many different meanings. It contains criticism against the rigid socialism of the communist
dictatorships but does not imply a rejection of socialism as a
practical strategy. Nor is it a question of a total repudiation
of Senator Bhör, and it ought to be pointed out that certain
sides of the boy, Elisa, and especially the governor are dubious
to say the least. One cannot miss the fact that the narrator feels
sympathy for the senator's indignation over social injustice and
human suffering. But the senator's despair over the collapse
of his political faith and the death wish born out of it are
definitely rejected. Senator Bhör's name has its root in a Swedish
verb which means "ought to" and it emphasizes a characteristic
of forced will. Much of the criticism directed toward him deals
with the fact that his feelings and ideas are exaggerated and
inflated. He uses gestures which are too large, and in this
perspective the melodramatic and thriller-like effects in the
novel receive a deeper meaning. It is clear that Gyllensten is
of the opinion that he does not at all have to react in the way
he does; there is instead a much more sober and objective way
of living—it is this message the senator's critics come with each
in turn. It is also as important that the senator's pathetic trait

is always presented as something childish. Through the narrator's analyses and comments it becomes clear that behind his angered protests lies a childish demand that the world should adapt itself according to him and his will. This is why he is so terrified when he does not recognize himself in the world and why he is offended at being so powerless. With some exaggeration it can be said that he sulks like a contrary child: "I don't want to be here!" (11). Thus in the end the senator's desperate death wish appears to have emerged from a childish level in him, and he turns out not at all unlike Gunnar in *Senilia*. According to the subtitle, *The Senator* is not only a melodrama, but also a didactic novel, and the novel's pedagogical significances lie most profoundly in the rejection of the senator's childish demands and reactions.

III   A Remarkable Death

The Death of Socrates is also a dialogue in its construction. The novel takes place during the last twenty-four hours of Socrates's life and the reader meets a relatively large number of characters: Socrates's young daughter Aspasia, the family's old servant, his son Lamprokles, Xanthippe, Aspasia's boyfriend, the prosecutor in the trial against Socrates and some of Socrates's philosopher friends. Each is allowed to speak in turn and they land in discussions with each other which are reminiscent of Plato's dialogues. The distinguishing trait of the novel is, however, the fact that the protagonist is physically absent. We only receive reports of Socrates's last day from the people who have visited him in prison, and when he makes his direct appearance in the novel it is as a corpse. Nevertheless, he is very present in the awareness of the other characters and determines their activities to a great degree. One of Aspasia's comments to the old servant is true of all of the people appearing: "We are both thinking of Father. We speak about him in secret..." (47 cont.). Therefore, many of the dialogues are directed toward Socrates and they describe the family's disturbed and critical reactions to his irrevocable decision to go to his death. In this way *The Death of Socrates* becomes a "trial" of Socrates within his own family, one which takes place alongside the public trial.

The first chapter of the novel sketches the background of the actions which follow. When Aspasia slowly wakes up in the family's humble house she half consciously transforms the sounds of the old servant's stone-cutting to bells announcing the arrival of the ship from Delos after its trip through the Greek islands. She has been longing for the sound of these bells. Her boyfriend is on the ship, and she is excited about what will happen when they meet again. But the bells also have a dark significance: Socrates was sentenced to death more than a month ago; however, by custom no executions take place in Athens while the ship is away, but upon its arrival the judgment will be carried out. Thus the ship from Delos becomes both a ship of life and of death. Later it will become clear that the ship actually arrived during the night.

As soon as Aspasia comes out in the early spring morning, the family's trial of Socrates begins. On the stairs she catches sight of a lizard which, with its wide mouth and bulging eyes, immediately makes her think of Socrates. This brief episode expresses all of her ambivalence to her father. On the one hand she is attached to him, and she develops her own view of life as a sensual adventure partly in relation to his ideas. What force in him makes people so attracted to him, she wonders. And her reply is that it is his bold and sober curiosity, which lets itself be blown toward strange coasts and unknown relationships and makes life worth living a thousand times and a thousand times again. But on the other hand it becomes clear further on in the novel that she cannot forgive her father the fact that by going to death he abandons her. This is nothing less than desertion and her criticism is expressed when she throws the Socrates-like lizard on the rubbish heap. The gesture forebodes her rejection of her father during his last day in life: instead of bidding him farewell in prison, she turns to her boyfriend and the adventures to which love tempts her.

Out in the courtyard the old servant is busy with his stone-cutting. He is worn out and almost broken by age and work, but he toils on quietly for the family's material existence. With an obvious reference to Socrates he tells Aspasia that someone who just goes around talking must have someone else tethered in his place. At first Aspasia thinks he is a milksop, but after a while she listens more carefully to his increasingly open criticism of Socrates. First the old man tells about his experiences of the war and pleads for "mercy for those who live" (28). But he becomes clearer when Aspasia suggests that Socrates, with his stubborn questions, wishes to hammer away all the confusing rubbish surrounding the person questioned so that the latter can in this way arrive at what is most important for himself. He replies that no one has any right to chop off a part of any other person and thus perhaps injure him, and when he develops his point of view his speech becomes powerful and passionate:

No honor and no truth, no city or building, no property, no alliance, no order, no anything is worth so much that one should raise his hand against an equal and do violence to him! Nothing, absolutely nothing is worth sacrificing someone's life—not even one's own. (41)

This is a statement of position which is directly aimed at Socrates who, in his choice to become a martyr, values philosophy more than his own life. Like Aspasia, the old servant definitely rejects Socrates's sacrificial death.

Aspasia's and the servant's conversation is, however, interrupted by Lamprokles's return from the prison where he has spent the night with his father and Xanthippe. In the exchange which follows between him and Aspasia it becomes clear that he has little interest in his father's philosophizing. He has never been able to give any tangible meaning to his father's words; instead they have been "breaths in the air" (52) for him. He is a farmer, he states emphatically, and the farmer's work has harsh rules which no clever talk can affect. Nevertheless, he is far from indifferent to his father. Although he sullenly announces that he has slept in prison, Aspasia realizes that he listened carefully to his parents' conversation during the night. At dawn, however, he sneaked away to his fiancée—an action which is parallel to Aspasia's absence from the last farewell to her father and her meeting with her boyfriend instead. It is tempting to see this act as a protest against the father in Lamprokles's case as well. As Aspasia observes, he bears a large grudge, and it is obvious that he feels disappointed in Socrates as a father.

Soon Xanthippe also comes home from prison with her youngest son on her back. Her attempts at persuading Socrates to flee have not succeeded, and she is sad. In the prison her anger has primarily been aimed at her husband's philosopher friends: "It was those cursed friends who always stole him away from those who needed *him* more than his *words*" (65). She does not place the guilt for Socrates's decision to go to death on his famous inner voice, but on his friends who seduced him into abandoning his home and family. Xanthippe sees something in Socrates for which his friends have no eyes. She has a little sculpture with her which he kneaded during a sleepless night and now has given to her on his last day of life. For her the sculpture is evidence of his distress in the face of death, and in it she sees a plea for help. She feels that he is calling for her and her strength. But it is just as clear that he is driven by another unfortunate instinct which tears him away from her. Therefore, in the end Xanthippe is powerless and not able to answer Socrates's dumb prayer for help.

With Xanthippe's return, all the members of the family are gathered together in the home, and all have had their first chance to speak. But as soon as Aspasia is sure that the ship from Delos has returned to port she sneaks away to meet her boyfriend, and the description of her flight to their meeting place is almost lyrical in character. She is borne by a jubilant freedom, and her eagerness makes the path run backward beneath her feet. Her tryst with her boyfriend under the open sky is also presented as an adventure. They discover their own and each other's bodies, make love with each other, and finally fall asleep. But even in their sleep they know that they have not received their fill and that the best is left for them. This scene, with all of its desire and light, is expressly in contrast to the narrow dark prison cell of Socrates. The contrast between Socrates and Aspasia becomes obvious: while he abstains from life for the sake of philosophy, she defiantly chooses the never-ending riches of sensual life.

The second main theme of *The Death of Socrates*, along with the family's coming to terms with Socrates, is included with the introduction of Aspasia's boyfriend. When the boy tells Aspasia about his trip aboard the ship from Delos he sketches a broad historical and political perspective of Greece in those days. "The war" which has been spoken of several times earlier in the novel is the Peloponnesian war between Sparta and Athens. This war was fateful, especially for Athens. Attica was devastated by the Spartans, the Athenians were forced to surrender their navy and to tear down the vitally important walls of the port city of Piraeus and in this way lost their hegemony in Greece. But it would also become clear that Sparta had exhausted its strength and thus the way southward lay open for Philip of Macedonia. In other words, in 399 B.C. the Athenian citizens had good reason to look forward to a dark future, and the boy's story is about this crisis. For him and his friends, the voyage aboard the ship has meant a political awakening. On the Greek islands they have seen the brutal traces of the Athenians' earlier policy of expansion for which the "arrogant construction" the Acropolis is a symbol (97). They have been met by hate and feel that the next war is on the doorstep. The boy's reply to these insights is violent protest and revolt: "I don't want to be a part of it, I won't go along with it!" (96). Together with his friends he instead dreams that a boldly sarcastic play could awaken the Athenians to an insight into their true situation and get them to hinder all further war activities. It is obvious that this radical criticism is in line with Socrates's questioning attitude, and the boy seems to a great degree to be a young Socrates.

But the political perspective is even broader. It is clear that in the situation of the Athenians Gyllensten sees a parallel to our times, and *The Death of Socrates* is, like Eyvind Johnson's reinterpretation of the *Odyssey* in *Strändernas svall* (1946) (Eng. tr. *Return to Ithaca* [1952]), a novel about the present.[8] He has woven clear associations to the mighty struggles of liberation of the third world from the colonial powers and the threat of atomic war from the 1950's into the boy's narration. But the main point of contact between then and now lies in the profound feeling of an approaching catastrophe of incredible proportions. Weapons became more and more terrifying, he writes in a passage which openly refers to the atomic weapons of our times; and the border line between victory and defeat is more and more meaningless (111). It is also clear that the conclusions which may be drawn about our times are the same the boy arrives at for his times. In a diary which Gyllensten wrote during the final stage of his work with *The Death of Socrates*, he summarized the political call of the novel in the following expressive way:

Catastrophe has stuck its snout up over the horizon and is staring humanity straight in the face, open and bold as Goya's Saturn. Here it is a question of saving what can be saved! Just get down on the ground, down among the cabbages, down in the grave or in the shelter, don't make trouble, take it easy and even easier! Until further notice.[9]

The boy's long story is also followed by a political perspective of another type. On their way home in the night Aspasia and the boy meet Meletos, the prosecutor, and his young lover. Meletos is drunk and tells more about the trial than what he actually thinks is wise. According to Gyllensten's way of writing history, the trial against Socrates has turned out completely wrong. Meletos's plan was to humble Socrates and in that way make him harmless. But by his provocative behavior Socrates has chosen sacrificial death and thus has made "a gesture of great and forceful seductiveness to the youth and their followers" (157). In his action against Socrates, Meletos is in conspiracy with Plato who is told to falsify Socrates's ideas in his writings, thereby disarming his revolt! The conflict between Socrates and Meletos could hardly have been more violent. Meletos sees the highest existing value in the state and its persistence, and his political activity is described in terms which leads one's thoughts to the political purging going on in modern times. As opposed to him, Socrates appears almost revolutionary with his individualist and critical attitude. Meletos's errand in the night reveals itself to be to find out in Socrates's home whether he really is dead or whether he managed to flee from prison at the last minute: in the latter case Meletos still has a chance to act, but in the former Socrates has won the game.

After this political discussion the perspective is once again shifted back to Socrates's family. One of Socrates's friends drives Meletos away and then follows Aspasia to the prison so that she may say her last farewell to her father. Earlier during the evening she declared that she could neither forgive nor forget Socrates, and she repeats her avowal to remember him to his dead body. The chapter—which is entitled "Motherliness"—is, however, dominated by Xanthippe and her last meeting with Socrates, which is described to Aspasia at her request by Kriton who has remained constantly present in the prison. Alone with her husband, Xanthippe once again pleads with him to use the possibility of escape from prison. She accuses him of being possessed with the idea of stamping his image on the world so that he will live on in history—a passion which she feels is lust for power. What really drives Socrates to death is what she calls god-man's desire to dissolve the boundaries of mortality. Xanthippe makes a definite judgment about this attraction to immortality. She finds it vain since god-man's existence in time is dependent upon the mortal's ability to keep his memory alive; and she finds it cruel because Socrates, with his martyr's death, creates a pattern for his equals in whose name they can do violence upon their fellow human beings. In opposition to Socrates's martyrdom she places instead "a quiet life among small things" (198)—the humble life of women, children, and animals, which leaves no traces in history but which offers a tender and caring love. Her last plea to her husband, the mother's, is: "come with me, and be like a child with me!" (119). The family's attitude to Socrates is to a great extent summarized in these words—both their criticism and their love. The weight of Xanthippe's words corresponds to the passion with which they are spoken, and her speech is in many respects the high point of the novel.

Aspasia, however, gets the last word in Socrates's death. When she slips out of the dark and disgusting prison she also leaves, at least for a while, the difficult experience of her father's desertion and death behind her. Outside she is met by blinding morning light and she is free. The light, the smells, the impressions of the senses, the aromas—everything fills her with a jubilant joy in existence and this experience is formulated in the song she sings. While it is true that our life is short, the song says, he who lives in the springtime tempts the clouds to bold sailing trips and games. *The Death of Socrates* ends on this song of praise to sensual life.

It is not easy to arrive at one simple conclusion about all of the dialogues and confrontations included in *The Death of Socrates*, and the novel must therefore be regarded as a fairly open discussion which moves in different directions. The novel ends, but without any pretense of delivering a complete and definite solution to the problems treated. Many of the tensions between the performing characters remain, and thus many questions also remain. The ambiguity is perhaps most obvious when it is a question of the picture of Socrates, which never really becomes solid and clear. Sven-Eric Liedman has suggested that Gyllensten's Socrates is neither Plato's builder of systems nor Xenophane's practical philosopher. According to Liedman, Gyllensten has instead seen Socrates through Kierkegaard's eyes, and he also emphasizes how close Socrates comes in this way to Gyllensten's own basic position.[10] As in Kierkegaard's thesis *On the Concept of Irony*, Socrates is, in Gyllensten's novel, primarily an ironist, who is always suspicious and questioning. He stubbornly asks his questions, but has no teaching of his own to present. It is important to emphasize that these sides of Socrates are treated with great sympathy in the novel, and through Aspasia's boyfriend Gyllensten presents Socrates's attitude as something current and relevant for the political situation of our times. As an eager critic in the spirit of Socrates, the boy appears as a significant supporter of Socrates.

But Socrates, the radical critic, voluntarily chooses to go to death; and it is on this point that Gyllensten is critical. Socrates's family joins in a chorus of irate, bitter and sorrowful voices against him and there is no doubt that Gyllensten is on their side. Socrates's desire to dissolve the barriers of mortality is unmasked as a more or less conscious game to win an immortal reputation. Furthermore, the question is whether or not Socrates has some of the same type of attraction to death that Senator Bhör demonstrated in *The Senator*. Perhaps one could even say that his repudiation of the corporeal is the source of a dissatisfaction for which he can see no other liberation than death. Against these dark instincts the members of Socrates's family instead plead for what Xanthippe calls the humble and simple little life, and after a while this emerges more clearly as the positive message of the novel. Of course they all demonstrate different sides of this life in small things: the old servant primarily emphasizes its mercifulness, Aspasia its sensualism, and Xanthippe its security. But for all of them this affirmation of the little life has its point directed against such heroic deeds as Socrates's sacrificial death. Throughout the novel Socrates's quest for immortality is opposed by the will to utilize the possibilities of life on earth.

In this way *The Death of Socrates* is not only a critical coming to terms with Plato's dialogues. It is certainly in conscious contrast to Plato that Gyllensten does not let Socrates himself describe the situation, but instead permits the family to speak. In this way their suspicion and criticism remains in contrast to Plato's glorification of Socrates's martyrdom. Thus the novel also receives a very pointed culturally critical significance. It is as though Gyllensten wished to show that there was something dark and destructive even in one of the most honored ideal figures of Western history. In the final analysis Socrates, too, joins the line of characters with destructive impulses and ambitions in the second period of Gyllensten's work.

IV   Desperadoes

The second period of Gyllensten's writing ended with a collection of short stories entitled *Desperadoes*, which in many ways is a summary of the novels he had finished. As Gyllensten mentions in the foreword, several of the short stories are studies for the novels—"attempts at finding and forming characters by whom I could be fooled so that I was tempted to load them with my stories and pictures" (17). One of them is from as far back as *Modern Myths*, two others were written in connection with *Infantilia*, but most of them belong to the preparatory work for *Senilia*. To begin with, this means that the motifs of the short stories are directly linked to the novels in process. For example, "The Problem of Three Bodies" describes a *menage à trois* similar to the one in *Infantilia*, and "Under the Earth" analyzes one of those tempting but dangerous invitations to love which recurs several times in *Senilia*. But most often the problems have another setting in the short stories and take somewhat different directions. One manifestation of such alter-

ations is the fact that several of the names from *Senilia* recur
in the short stories, but the people bearing them are nevertheless
different in important respects from the characters in the novel.
And conversely, a few recurrent figures from the novels have
received names which do not occur in the novels.[11] In this way
the short stories stand for themselves at the same time as they
prepare the way for a dialogue with the novels. The last two
stories in the collection differ, however, from these stories in
that they are preparatory studies for two of Gyllensten's coming
novels; and they point out the directions he would come to
take in his subsequent writing.

But even more important than the relationship in motifs is
the fact that Gyllensten so clearly established the basic questions
of the novels of the second period in *Desperadoes*. The central
concept is already revealed in the title of the collection, and
the relationship is made clear in the extensive foreword. In a
dialogue with an imagined and fairly critical reader, Gyllensten
declares, consciously using paradoxical terms, that he has most
firmly repudiated convictions which are too firmly established.
He thinks he can especially distinguish between two groups
of desperadoes: those who are in despair because they have
no faith to cling to, and those who are filled with bitterness
because not everyone else shares the same convictions as they
do. In the latter case the bitterness is directly based upon too
much conviction, and in the former it is the lack of a strong
conviction which gives birth to the despair. But both of these
groups of desperadoes land on the wrong foot in existence
because they ask too much. Gyllensten sets up his own epistemological view in contrast to theirs: philosophies of life and
explanations of existence are images which may be compared
to maps. Therefore they are tools which we use to orient ourselves in life, but they are not reality itself. Anyone who asks
of a philosophy that it be an absolute authority is simply asking
too much. Gyllensten himself demands no guarantees in support
of his own existence and pleads for a more humble way of
relating to reality. Once again with a paradoxical turn he speaks
of a kind of levity, which means "believing in something as if
one didn't believe in it, and living in the world as if one didn't
live in it" (17).

In accord with these ideas, the short stories then describe a whole line of desperadoes in different situations and conditions. In "Zarathustra, the Sunday Hunter," the main character is a musician on holiday. He has got up early and is on his way up to a little cottage on a mountain. A warbling bird reminds him of the composition he is working on, and he is gripped with fear at the thought of not being able to complete it. Soon, however, he is captured by the rhythm of the walk and impressions from nature move him deeply. His steps grow longer, he is filled more and more by an ecstatic feeling of strength and experiences as in a crescendo a dizzying wordless surrender. But the experience collapses immediately. In his recklessness he tramps right on the back of a toad and it bursts to pieces. Suddenly he realizes how tired he is, and he lapses into a kind of emotional hangover. A wave of loathing washes over him; he sees that he has come into a ravaged part of the forest with only branches and stones, and he cannot understand how he will ever find the strength to continue. The reference to Nietzsche is important. In his ecstatic strength the musician imagines that he is a superman: a genius who with invincible strength creates his own orbit—not just the image of a god, but a god himself. The march up to the top of the mountain expresses his will to be in control of reality. But this illusive feeling of strength rests, in fact, on a profound anxiety. His cramp-like way of holding on to his composition shows that he does not dare to expose himself to the changeable and unknown in life. The goal of his striving is to place a familiar pattern over reality, and when this pattern does not hold he lands in the grips of despair. Perhaps his intoxicated dream of divine strength has as its source a childish refusal to accept the fact that his power over reality is limited.

If this anxiety over a changeable reality is one of the characteristics of Gyllensten's desperadoes, another is the destructivity they develop. In "Archaic Rite" three actors put on a gruesome performance. A father and a mother dress their son in a straightjacket and lay him in a coffin. Then the mother shoves a long mouthpiece further and further down his throat. It is more and more difficult for him to breathe, and the sounds which come out of the instrument finally become inhuman cries of anguish.

It is only when he is practically smothered that the seance is broken. This rite is archaic in that it gives form to a mythical pattern of rebirth, which may be found in most of the great mythological systems. In the words of the father, the goal of the sacrifice of the son is purity and transformation. For the mumbling public a Word shall be created and a Voice sent. But the contrast to the rebirth to a new life which takes place in the ancient myths could hardly be greater. With vulgar sexual gestures the actor's grotesque performance instead moves toward an orgiastic climax. It is not only a deliberate game, the purpose of which is to excite a strong and inebriating experience, it is also a tantalizing game with death: an attempt to find a stimulation in the boundary areas of death which is stronger than what life seems to be able to offer. The price for this ecstasy is the appalling anxiety over death which the son must suffer.

But *Desperadoes* also summarizes Gyllensten's reserved position in relation to these desperate impulses. In "A Slap Across the Face" two childhood friends go out to a bar and consume a fair amount of alcohol. One of them is called the Count and can control his drunkenness. The other goes under the name of the Boy and soon speaks pathetically and sentimentally about one of their friends who has become mentally ill. The Count ridicules him more and more openly and finally the Boy throws his drink in his face. But the meeting between them has important consequences in that the very same day the Count sends two letters off to the Boy. In the first of them he violently accuses the Boy of using dissolution as an aphrodisiac. But the second letter is even more important. In it he rejects a whole line of ideals and values. Using a style with only capital letters and in a strongly controlled anger he accuses Christ because he crowned death and suffering as the way to salvation, love because everywhere it is only lust for power, truth because it does not permit other truths alongside of it, fidelity because it cannot permit changes, and finally security because it turns into despair when disappointed (100 cont.). It is always a question of very pointed formulations which almost appear as antithetical commandments. But the significance is clear: even the values which we by tradition place highest in our culture have dangerous and destructive elements.

In this way *Desperadoes* not only permits a solid perspective backward on Gyllensten's novels of the second period: in their anxiety and destructivity, Gunnar in *Senilia*, Antonin Bhör in *The Senator*, and Socrates in *The Death of Socrates*, can all fittingly be called desperadoes; and the novels are forceful settlements with them. Furthermore, the short stories demonstrate clearly that his criticism points in two directions. On the one hand he comes to terms with a whole collection of emotions and needs like jealousy, the experience of being small and powerless, and a violent lust for power. These feelings are often characterized as childish, the desperado is in fact regarded as a child, and the concepts "child" and "desperado" coincide to a great extent. On the other hand criticism is directed toward a line of ideas and ideals which, seen more closely, appear to be dangerous and destructive. It is in the interplay of these childish feelings and these dangerous ideas that Gyllensten's desperadoes emerge: the feelings receive their direction from the ideas, the ideas find their nourishment in the feelings, and therefore this whole game must be exposed. It is also important to emphasize how far-reaching Gyllensten's criticism is. In the foreword to *Desperadoes* Gyllensten declares: "I do not like desperadoes" (9). But this is a formulation which is really charged with understatement and the vehemence with which Gyllensten dismisses his desperadoes is palpable. The basis for his at once psychological and ideological criticism may be said to be an elementary and radical humanism which passionately guards the life of the individual human being from destructive forces both from within and from without.

Still, *Desperadoes* is the endpoint of the second period of Gyllensten's authorship. There is no mistake that the settlement with these desperadoes was a response to a deep need and was necessary. But the reserved and stoic attitude to life would turn out to be untenable in the long run. Perhaps one could say that it was too clearly defensive in character. The whole point of the mobilization was to disarm destructive impulses and ideas. But in a less stressed situation the need for more positive goals and strategies of action make themselves known. Gyllensten's authorship would from here on once again come to follow new lines.

CHAPTER 4

Iconoclasm

THE first phase of Gyllensten's authorship was followed by a radical process of reorientation. After the second phase he was apparently also involved in conscientious and time-consuming efforts to find new directions for his writing. *The Death of Socrates* was published in 1960. Two years later *Desperadoes* marked the endpoint of the second period, and it seems that the process of reorientation had already begun. According to Gyllensten himself, the two novels which introduced the third period of his work were originally thought of as one novel: *Cain's Memoirs* was at first planned as a part of *Juvenilia*, but grew to such size that it became a novel on its own.[1] Thus there is a very close connection between *Cain's Memoirs* and *Juvenilia*, and furthermore *Juvenilia* must therefore belong to the introductory part of the third period. *Cain's Memoirs* was published in 1963, and *Juvenilia* was not completed until 1965. Gyllensten's break away from the positions of the second period was no easy, painless thing.

But the third period was also preceded by two brief but important declarations of policy. In 1962 Gyllensten published two chapters of *Cain's Memoirs* in *BLM*, Bonnier's literary magazine. In an introductory note he explained that in *The Senator* and in *The Death of Socrates* he had presented strategies of reason, but that there was also, in these novels, the latent counter-polemic that our images of reality can become prisons which must be torn down if life and reality are to reveal themselves. He also said that he had been making formal experiments in that direction for a couple of years and was in the process of seeking "a narrative position in the collage method" for himself.[2] Two years later Gyllensten published a few sections of *Juvenilia* in *BLM* and presented a more extensive description of this collage method in a new note:

These pieces belong to a novel I have been working on for the past few years. It is a kind of collage-novel. It consists of different literary fragments, literary incarnations, which an anonymous author (Cain) creates and puts together. He only exists in these incarnations which he rejects individually. In order to escape from the limitations, the prison, by which he feels bound, because his own force constantly refers him back to his own memory, his own knowledge, his own words and other such things which he recognizes as his own, he attempts to change incarnations, to exchange forms and juxtapose conflicting fragments.[3]

It should be noted that Gyllensten speaks of "a kind of collage-novel." As a matter of fact, the collage method he uses in the novels is not orthodox. He does not utilize already existing texts of documentary character or from other authors. The material he uses to construct his collages are texts which he has written himself. One could say that he works with the method of composition of the collage without making use of its technique of quoting. In somewhat different words than in Gyllensten's note, the form of collage-novel he works with can thus be described as a collection of different types of texts which he has first written and then put together. It may seem that this collage method is too unorthodox to merit its name, and the way in which Gyllensten works the texts together to relatively harmonious units in the later novels of the third period could perhaps be better characterized as montage. But it is clear that Gyllensten wished to give the novels from the introductory stage of the period a form which is similar to that of the collage in art. With its disparate and often abruptly ending texts, *Juvenilia* primarily leads one's thoughts to that type of collage which consists of bits of text and pictures torn out of newspapers and magazines. In both cases it is a question of constructions of bits and pieces.

The concept of collage becomes more than adequate if one looks at the deeper meaning Gyllensten attributes to the collage. The significance of the collage form is also altered in the novels from the later part of the period. But in the novels which introduce the collage period it is clear that the collage form is intimately linked with the undertaking which is the basis of the novels. In the second note in *BLM*, Gyllensten declared that

his aim in setting up the conflicting fragments against each other
was to be able to discover a reality beyond one's own limitations
"approximately as the expression in a collage grows out of the
composition of heterogenous fragments which have been torn
out of their contexts and received other, unimagined, functions."[4]
In the same way an important link is established in *Juvenilia*
between the collage form and what Gyllensten, with another
central concept, calls iconoclasm. He uses this originally religious
term in a figurative sense: iconoclasm for him is no longer a
breaking of the images of God in a literal sense, but rather
an intellectual process, the goal of which is to break the images
and patterns with which we interpret reality in order to make
new experiences and insights possible. A passage from *Juvenilia*
demonstrates how close the concepts of collage and iconoclasm
are to each other—an artist is speaking:

I have landed in Cain's situation, the iconoclast's—I feel a forceful
need (yes, excuse me, as imperative as a natural need) to destroy
my pictures, and worse: my whole way of making pictures and
images and to create, the whole of my language in the word's most
pretentious sense, my antecedents. (214)

In other words, the iconoclast's attempts to break the images of
the reality he creates correspond to the broken collage form. In
both instances it is a case of bursting through existing patterns
to create new patterns with the pieces. The collage seems to
be the correct artistic means of expression for the iconoclast to
such a great extent that one is almost tempted to call the
collage a special form of iconoclasm.

In this perspective, iconoclasm in the collage period's introductory phase appears to be Gyllensten's means of conquering
the reserved attitude of the second period. He was no longer
attempting to recognize and disarm destructive impulses. Instead, he now wished to discover new experiences and insights.
Nor was the collage form congenial with this quest for iconoclasm
on a general level alone. In *Juvenilia* the idea that old forms
bind us to well-trained patterns of thought is presented several
times, and more specifically, Gyllensten certainly used the
collage form in the introductory phase of the period to break

away and free himself from the ironic narrative attitude of the novels from the second period.

I *In the Guise of Cain*

To begin with, *Cain's Memoirs* seems like a direct prolongation of Gyllensten's previous novels. The subject of the novel is a heretical sect from the first centuries after the birth of Christ, whose members worshiped Cain and therefore called themselves Cainites. What gives the novel its special mark is the narrative approach which is so consistently used: Gyllensten permits an anonymous historicist to tell about the Cainites, and the influence of Thomas Mann's ironic diction is very apparent in the tone of this narrator. It is quite clear that the chronicle deals with serious things, and one cannot miss the fact that the chronicler feels profound sympathy for the Cainites. The narrative tone, however, is almost even more ironic and bantering than in *Senilia*. When the chronicler discusses the scholarly researchers' interpretations of the Cainite's fragmentary writings especially he develops a playfulness which almost upsets the game. In one of the chapters, for example, he tells about a cashbook which had been found with personal notes in the margins. The slant of the letters and the uneven handwriting suggest that the person who wrote was left-handed. In the pages of this cashbook lay a book of ideas which apparently was kept by the same person. Three of the paragraphs of this book deal with how a person loses an arm and seem to confirm the hypothesis that the writer was left-handed. But then the chronicler abruptly changes his argument. First of all, the information given in the three paragraphs is conflicting and permits no definite conclusion as to how the writer lost his arm. Secondly, one cannot with certainty claim that the characteristics of the handwriting truly suggest that the writer was left-handed! This extreme uncertainty as to how the writings ought to be interpreted corresponds to the Cainite's view of human beings' knowledge of the nature of reality.

The bantering chronicler first narrates the history of the Cainites. The Cainites lived in a smaller city in upper Egypt which was called Diospolis Parva (The Small City of God), and worked as businessmen. Business was booming during the reign of Emperor Hadrianus and the significance of the city was so great that a Roman garrison was stationed there. On merchant routes through the desert caravans from Africa came loaded with all conceivable kinds of wares and from there were sent on to different parts of the Roman Empire. While it is true that the Cainites were a religious sect with their own views of God and were surrounded by a long line of sects with other views, one of their most characteristic traits was their conciliatoriness and tolerance. On the basis of their experience as businessmen, they had come to the conclusion that the best thing for coexistence between different peoples was to "level those differences which can be levelled, and increase those similarities which can be increased, while one tactfully leaves everything else to its own without paying it too much attention" (7; Eng. tr. 5). When Diospolis Parva was at the height of its boom about thirty families were members of the Cainite sect.

Soon, however, things went bad for the Cainites. With the fall of the Roman Empire, business declined in Diospolis Parva, and the garrison left town. Parts of the population moved to other places in the empire in the hopes of better means of living and the remainder slowly sank into poverty. Even the climate worsened: the winds blew hotter and hotter, and the desert ate at the fields and gardens. Added to this, many members of the growing Christian sect moved to the city. The Cainites had sometime earlier been the victims of violence on the part of the raw Roman soldiers in the garrison. But this was nothing compared to the persecution they had to suffer at the hands of the Christians who, as opposed to the Cainites, took advantage of every opportunity to oppress people who thought differently and to force them to adopt their own preaching. Several of the Cainite families fled from Diospolis Parva to avoid persecution and settled in a deteriorating suburb outside of the town. Finally they lived in caves in the ground and were on their way to losing their use of the Greek language. It was in this distressed situation that they wrote down oral tales and stories which had been the property of the sect. In the face of their downfall they wished to be reminded of who they were.

During his narration, the chronicler also describes the Cainites' ideas about and views on the world. Here it is primarily a question of three complexes of ideas which are linked to each other. In the first place the Cainites adopted a principally skeptical attitude as regards the possibility of arriving at an absolutely certain knowledge of reality. They had noted, the chronicler writes, that the truth is shy and usually only reveals itself masked and in disguise. These masks are all imperfect and misshapen, but they are nevertheless useful and respectable helpers against the confusion and affliction which otherwise lies in wait—it is not difficult to recognize Gyllensten's own epistemological views in these comments. But the idea that it would be possible to seek something behind all of these masks also is glimpsed: "Truth must be sought behind human beings' images of truth" (86; Eng. tr. 57). Furthermore, the Cainites in many respects have a pessimistic view of life. The fate of Diospolis Parva made them aware that what happens in life does not consider the wishes and fears of men. They know that they shall die themselves and that insight has laid sorrow and bitterness upon their spirits. They also understand that time is bad and unfavorable to human beings' attempts to hold their own in the world. Finally, on the basis of these conditions, they draw the conclusion that the god who created the world must be evil and they reject him. It was in his characteristic of rebel against God that Cain gave his name to the sect. And this profound mistrust on the part of the Cainites of the nature of the world lies in line with the reserved attitude toward life in Gyllensten's novels from the second period.

But *Cain's Memoirs* does not only consist of the ironic chronicles. In the latter half of the novel the chronicler introduces excerpts from the previously mentioned existing writings of the Cainites and it becomes more and more clear that there is a tension between these texts and the chronicle. The contrast is already clear if one regards the style: in the stories and tales which are related, the bantering tone of the chronicle, with few exceptions, is completely absent. In opposition to the chronicler's distance and reserve is the open and direct expression of feelings of sorrow, bitterness and anger. There is a completely naked and almost unbearable despair in some of the stories. It is as if the emotions the chronicler so definitely keeps under control now can flow freely. The stories also distinguish themselves from the chronicle in form. According to the comments of the chronicler, only parts of the writings of the Cainites have been kept and the writings which were discovered were in very bad condition. He firmly underlines that the remaining texts are only fragments of the original writings, which are to a great extent incomplete and fragmentary. Several of the stories he presents are also only fragments: they begin and end in the middle of a sentence and the story is not completed. In this way the excerpts from the writings of the Cainites build a collage in Gyllensten's use of the concept; and this collage appears, against the background of the supervisory chronicler, much more open and suggestive in character. But most important is that the ideas which are formulated in the stories of the Cainites lead in another direction than the chronicle. The point of departure is the same for both the chronicle and the stories, but the expedient suggested in the stories is not ironic distance. If one regards the chronicle as a narrative framework around the collage composed of the Cainite's writings, then one could say that the collage finally breaks through the framework of the chronicle.

The stories the chronicler presents are not completely uniform. A few of the narratives have a sharp edge directed at the tendency of the Christians to interpret everything which happens for the best. In one of them a pious Jew is refused night lodgings in an inhospitable village and instead camps out in a nearby ravine. During the night the wind extinguishes his lantern and a wild animal makes off with his rooster and his donkey. In the morning he sees that during the night the village was ravaged by robbers and understands that he was saved thanks to the fact that neither the lantern, rooster nor donkey revealed his camping place. What at first seemed to be his misfortune in the end turned out to be his salvation, and he feels strengthened in his view that God really is good. This conclusion is, however, definitely rejected as an infatuation: even if the pious Jew was saved, the fact remains that the whole population of the village was slaughtered. Something of the chronicler's irony remains in this demonstration of the evil of the world. But the polemics are absent in several of the stories. Some of them are myths of creation with well-known themes. One of them describes how the first human being is born out of the earth and bitterly complains about nature's mastery of men. Other stories paint the pain and torture of human life in somber words. A few lines which introduce one of the brief fragments are characteristic: "A good wind always blows towards Hades, though the trip may seem to be roundabout" (74; Eng. tr. 49).

The most significant excerpts from the writings of the Cainites, however, consist of three fragments dealing with the figure who gave his name to the sect. These three fragments recollect Cain's fate in three different versions, which both complement and contradict each other. The first fragment is short (108 cont.; Eng. tr. 72 cont.). As in the Bible, Cain is a man of the fields and Abel is a great hunter. Abel sacrifices the quarry he has captured to God, and God reveals Himself to him and calls him His son. Cain's sacrifice of ripe barley and sweet fruit does not, however, suit God's taste. God turns away from him, and life to Cain seems poor in everything but toil. In anger over his brother's savagery and recklessness Cain finally kills Abel; and now, at last, God reveals Himself to him: tempted by the blood from Abel's body, God climbs down to the fratricide and puts His mark upon him. But Cain is filled with loathing for life. He turns away from the evil god and seeks the rest which is hidden behind the face of the god.

The second fragment is also short (144 cont.; Eng. tr. 97 cont.) and describes Cain's life after the fratricide. Through the murder Cain was able to see the wrath in the eyes of the evil god. The context is not completely clear, but the sense is probably that the god who only pays attention to Cain when he becomes a fratricide cannot be good to men. Therefore Cain goes out into the forest and lives among the wild animals. He drives the memory of men from his heart and forgets the language and skills of men. Much later, by mistake, he is taken as a quarry; and the two hunters find him on his face in the bushes. He has horns on his forehead and resembles for the most part an ape. But when the hunters turn him around they find an old man's face, and they are filled with horror. They despise him and bury him like an animal which has died by itself. At the very end it is said that they do not understand that he has broken away from mankind because there is something he could not endure. But there the text is cut, and what Cain could not endure is never formulated clearly.

It is the third fragment which is most significant, and which also receives special weight through its placement last in the novel. As opposed to the two other fragments, it is written in the first person. Gyllensten calls it Cain's testament, and for twenty pages he permits Cain to give a complete description of his life up to and including the fratricide. The first thing Cain remembers is something green and big and shining. Afterward he understands that it was the leaves above him and that his father and mother were in flight with him. They lived a nomadic life and were driven by necessity to seek one living place after another. But after a while Cain's father rebelled against this necessity. He began to cultivate the earth, tried to tame the beasts, and instead of huts and caves he built them houses. They were still forced to move a few times, but in the end they could hold their own against both the storms and the droughts. Using one of the central concepts from *Senilia*, Cain notes: "Father forced evil to bow under his cane" (168; Eng. tr. 114).

As soon as Cain grows up he, too, goes to agricultural labor. The tribulations of the nomadic life are only memories for him, but the goal of all of his striving is that that hard, evil life may never return. The proverb he lives by is, "he who can, must raise his strength against torment!" (181; Eng. tr. 123). And outwardly he is making progress. With patience and resourcefulness he gets the earth to feed them year after year. But as a mature man he is seized by spleen. Once again, using terms which go back to *Senilia*, he sees the remainder of his life as an endless repetition of days which are exactly alike. The constant toil has no other goal than toil itself, and in the long run it is still not enough. He sees that in the end death will destroy the protection his strength raises and slaughter both men and animals. Those who live seem to him to live in vain.

Abel is in obvious contrast to Cain. As a youth Abel refuses to go into a life of agriculture together with Cain and the rest of the people on the farm. Instead he runs free in the forest, hunts, and sacrifices to a stone image in a cave in the mountain. There is something wild and cruel about him: once Cain sees him stab a young wild boar and fiercely put his mouth over the spouting blood. As a contrast to Cain's life of hard labor, his existence is filled with pleasure and sensuality. Cain curses his savagery several times and encourages him to begin working on the farm, but Abel only ridicules his words. In one of these confrontations he hisses back at Cain: "Why do you live?" (181; Eng. tr. 123).

It is this conflict which leads up to the fratricide. One morning in the autumn Cain goes off to Abel's cave. With his hoe he breaks the image of the false god and scratches out the pictures Abel has painted on the walls. When he is surprised by Abel he hits him hard on the forehead with the hoe, and this act seems to be done half in anger and half in self-defense. But after the killing he is struck by a violent dizziness, and he falls to the ground beside his brother. The whole of that day, the following night, and even the next day he lies there in great anxiety. He realizes that the image of his dead brother has become so imprinted on him that he will never be able to get rid of it. Nor does he dare to return to the farm. In the end he goes out to the forest and hides himself from people like a wild animal.

This story is to a certain extent in line with the ironic chronicler's presentation of the dogmas and attitudes of the Cainites. Cain's hard labor to hold his own, his spleen, and his rejection of Abel's worship of false gods—all of this fits together with the Cainite's practical care of people, their pessimistic view of the conditions of life, and their skeptical attitude to the many teachings about the world and God. Cain, the farmer, rightly appears as a figure honored by the Cainites. But at the same time, it is clear that Cain goes beyond the Cainite's view of life with the fratricide. It is not only that the fratricide directly repudiates the tolerance and conciliatoriness which the ironic chronicler so eloquently attributed to the Cainites. What happens to him in the fratricide is that he turns his back on the agricultural life. Even earlier his satiation showed that hard labor did not give his life enough content, and with the fratricide he definitely leaves his previous life. Thus within the novel the

story of Cain functions as a denial of the durability of the reserved attitude of the ironic chronicler.

This point becomes even more clear if one looks at the concrete description of the fratricide. There is no doubt that Gyllensten presents the events in the cave as an act of iconoclasm. When Cain splits Abel's stone image he is literally breaking the image of a false god. But breaking the image also fits together with the killing itself: Abel's blood wets the pieces of the image and splashes over the scratched pictures on the walls. After the killing Cain thinks that the images sneer at him, and he experiences the scratches on the walls as strange marks and spells. But this iconoclastic event lies far from the Cainites' purely intellectual attempts to break the masks of the gods in order to gain insight into what lies behind. What Cain does is far more radical: one could say that in actuality he breaks out of his agricultural life. After the killing, his previous life lies in bits and pieces and there is no return. Through this tormenting experience he is ushered into something new, and it is in this respect that the third fragment on Cain breaks up the attitude of the ironic chronicler. Thus it follows that the longest story about Cain finishes the novel without allowing the ironic chronicler another chance to speak.

II A Decampment

About halfway through *Juvenilia*, there is an important reference to *Cain's Memoirs*—though in the playful way which is reminiscent of the bantering chronicler's attitude to the labor of the researchers in interpreting the writings of the Cainites.[5] In a letter to Gyllensten, one of the novel's main characters sketches a literary project which is a direct description of *Cain's Memoirs* (96 cont.). He says that he has received a present from his ex-wife, an old manuscript for which she paid a large amount of money to a French antique dealer. It consists of about twenty pages of parchment with Greek text and, according to the antique dealer, it was written by a gnostic sect in a little village in upper Egypt. The letter-writer had allowed a specialist to translate the text and been fascinated by "the holes in the texts, the faults in interpretation and especially the bizarre aroma of authenticity and falsification at the same time" (99). He plans eventually to donate the manuscript to a scientific library, but until then he wants to use it for his own writing. In the letter he turns to Gyllensten with a request to cooperate on this project.

This playful construction hints at Gyllensten's original plan with the text which later became *Cain's Memoirs*. There are a few texts in *Juvenilia* which are presented as the protagonist's literary attempts, and it is certain that the story of the Cainites was thought of as one such attempt.[6] But even more important is the function the letter has in *Juvenilia* in the novel's final form: with a direct reference back to *Cain's Memoirs* the letter points out that Cain is also a central figure in *Juvenilia*. This point is also demonstrated in the way that Cain constantly turns up in the diary entries and reflections of the three main characters in *Juvenilia*, and they identify themselves so closely to him a few times that they call themselves Cain. The effect achieved in this way is that behind the main characters one finds the image of Cain as it was painted in *Cain's Memoirs*. One can say that *Juvenilia* is about a few people living in the present, all of whom exist in Cain's situation in life.

However, due to the fragmented collage form of *Juvenilia*, this pattern is not crystallized until later. *Juvenilia* consists of a little more than sixty sections of varying length and form. In several of the pieces the protagonist of the novel is referred to in the third person and in a line of other pieces the characters themselves narrate in the first person. Furthermore, there are several parts which consist of the working notes and diary entries of the main characters, some of their literary attempts, and a number of the letters they write—but most often never send away. Finally one finds a few odd texts: a few intense dialogues, two *curriculae vitæ*, and a doctor's report. Characteristic of the collage in *Juvenilia* is that these different texts are mixed with each other in such a way that one form of presentation is often abruptly succeeded by another. And as in *Cain's Memoirs*, a few of the texts are fragmentary in the sense that they begin and end in the middle of a sentence. Finally, the impression of fragmentation is reinforced by the fact that the main characters have certain mutual relationships but still are never really confronted with each other. In this way the texts of *Juvenilia* may give the impression of being the remains of a novel with a conventional plot which was broken into bits.

The three main characters of the novel meet the reader through these broken texts, and their portraits are never really completed. Torsten Mannelin is a doctor with a private practice as well as being the supervisor of a home for retarded children. He was divorced several years ago and lives alone. On the side, he eagerly devotes himself to writing essays and stories. Evert von Pierow has worked in a bank, but has devoted himself totally to his art for the past few years. As a kind of liberation for his art, he sometimes writes vulgar and obscene stories. He, too, is divorced or, in any case, no longer lives with his wife. Eric Vickler, finally, lives almost completely without social relationships. He is an engineer but no longer works. Apparently he has earned a large amount of money on a plastics factory which later collapsed and now is living on his assets. He is a bachelor, and there does not seem to be any woman in his life. The aura of loneliness which surrounds him is strongly reinforced by the fact that he is an epileptic. All of these men have apartments in a section of Östermalm where Strindberg once lived, and in their lonely walks one can perhaps see a reference to Strindberg's description of his isolation after his divorce from Harriet Bosse in the short novel *Alone*.

Later on, however, it turns out that these three persons also share significant similarities on a deeper level, and it is now that Cain peeps out from behind them. In the first place, all three express the somber pessimism which grips Cain in the concluding fragment of *Cain's Memoirs*. In the beginning of *Juvenilia*, Mannelin goes out for a morning walk. It is autumn, the air is chilly and clear; and he notices that it is a beautiful day. But the morning papers have reminded him of the violence and destruction in the world, and the beauty is poisoned for him. The future, to him, is a dark cone which becomes inexorably narrower the further in one comes and which ends in death and destruction: "Death is the only certain thing; destruction is the answer of the future" (10). Von Pierow and Vickler express similar somber statements on the supreme power of death and violence and, like Mannelin, they ask themselves how they will be able to endure.

These general attitudes are also given an obtrusive concretion in the novel. Mannelin has a son who is an incurable spastic, and in the beginning of the novel the birth which caused the injury is rolled up again and again in a tormenting dream. He sees a bluish-red and swollen arm sticking out and then the swollen head puffs up like a boil beside the arm. Finally the boy lies limp and gasping for breath on the midwife's sheet, and it is only after awhile that he decides to live. Mannelin has arranged for the boy as well as he can, and he makes his contribution for the retarded children in the home in the hopes that others will care for his son after his death. But he cannot take away his son's injury, and at bottom he feels impotent. Mannelin's son reappears in another form as the retarded girl who sometimes rings both von Pierow's and Vickler's doorbells. Once when her parents have a party von Pierow finds her locked in a supply room. She whines like a little animal, tears and mucous run down into her mouth, and her eyes are filled with senseless fear. There is a wet patch on the rug under her, and she stinks of old and fresh urine. Von Pierow takes her into his apartment, washes her, gets her to sleep and takes her back to her parents the next day. After this episode the girl begins to reach for von Pierow in the stairs and to cling to his legs. But when in an anonymous letter he is accused of obscene behavior with a minor he flees abroad to "rethink" (154).

The fact that it is not in their power to help these two injured children fills the three main characters with anger and bitterness. "There is no shield against the future—love builds houses of cards—care and attention draw friendly spirals in the sand— but everything men create shall be destroyed," Mannelin states in a characteristic turn of phrase (10). But even though they are not able to do anything, they cannot forget the children. The suffering in the world cannot either be relieved or reconciled, but they must nevertheless endure it somehow. Vickler's prayer for freedom from sympathy on the last page of the novel must be read in this emotional context. The sympathy he speaks of attacks him like a pain which would become unendurable if it lasted long. It thrusts through him like a stiff finger through a mushroom and rides him like an attack of cramps. But since he is impotent in the face of evil, who can blame him if he seeks liberation from pain? Therefore his prayer, and that of the two other main characters, is formulated somewhat paradoxically: "O free me from love for man!" (228).

Furthermore, Mannelin, von Pierow, and Vickler all experience the same type of spleen which struck Cain in the concluding fragment of *Cain's Memoirs*. They are all middle-aged and find what is happening to them in their lives only too familiar. A claustrophobic sensation of being locked into worn-out positions in life runs throughout the novel. In one of his diary entries Mannelin is so full of distaste for himself that he writes about himself in the third person: "He does not satisfy me, I am losing my appetite, my eyes lose their shine in his nearness; sleep, death opens itself like a yawn" (88). In other contexts this stifling familiarity is presented as being enclosed in human categories in general. Vickler has an aquarium, and on one occasion he compares his own encapsulation in human concepts and prejudices to the fish's imprisonment behind the glass. Another reality can be imagined on the other side of the glass, but not really grasped. As in *Cain's Memoirs*, Gyllensten here refers back to certain ideas in *Senilia*. Mannelin's father is very similar to Torsten Lerr's father, and from him he has learned that insight can transform the world to a familiar and secure place of abode. But in *Juvenilia* this attitude has led to a cramped and unfruitful situation; and in a retrospective polemic with his father, Mannelin instead claims that this familiarity must be dissolved.

It is not only that the situation of the three protagonists is similar to Cain's, but the strategies they design are also based on the interpretation of the figure of Cain given in *Cain's Memoirs*. Mannelin, von Pierow, and Vickler are all in a searching phase and try approaches in several directions. One of the main themes in their diary entries is that they, like Cain after the fratricide, wish to turn away from human beings. In a brief section toward the end of the novel a freedom which can be conquered by leaving "human claims and cries" is mentioned. One can attain this freedom by seeking out "the loneliness which exists within, the empty room where no one else takes part in one's existence, where even one's own past has no power nor significance" (225). This idea, which recurs in several places in *Juvenilia*, is that there is a deep level in the personality which the human language does not reach with all of its incitements and demands. There we are free in the sense that the many norms and claims which surround us have no power over us. By going into this hole within ourselves we can attain a liberation which is both endurable and fruitful.

Von Pierow especially formulates this attempt to reject the human in more brutal terms. In a literary discussion with Mannelin he criticizes Samuel Beckett's misanthropy for being too pompous and sentimental in its despair. He recommends instead true misanthropy, which means indifference and disdain for the dignity of human beings. Von Pierow refers to a few quarreling old hags he saw as a boy as representatives of this misanthropy. When they had heaped all conceivable curses upon each other they went on to the most extreme insult: they pulled their skirts over their heads, crouched down and turned their backsides to each other. These hags return in his slogan of "turning one's back on that which is human" and also give a hint as to the meaning of the slogan. Against the bombastic human claims he places obscenity as a means of freeing oneself, and this is why he writes his pornographic stories. In the end, the obscene gestures serve the purpose of taking him out to "the bestial and paradisical freedom which is outside of humanity" (167). As the formulation suggests, this striving to reject human things primarily has to do with a liberation from the torturing sympathy.

The second main theme in the three protagonists' diary entries is iconoclasm, which is presented as an act of vital necessity. As in *Cain's Memoirs*, the goal of iconoclasm is to smash existing images and patterns; but in *Juvenilia* there are several attempts to make the significance of iconoclasm more precise. In his letter to Gyllensten, Mannelin declares that with his words and concepts he attempts to form a tenable image of the world in which he lives. But he also confesses a tendency to asceticism which threatens to impoverish his experiences and to simplify his problems. Therefore it is important for him "to break up the patterns in which I am dressed, and to expand the space

in myself" (95). Here it is primarily a question of breaking
away from habitual ways of thinking and forms of experience.
But von Pierow especially emphasizes that this cannot be
merely an intellectual process which leaves the actor untouched.
On the contrary, he states that it is just as important for him
to break down the ideas he has about himself: "The image of
myself must also be attacked and re-formed—this is the most
difficult task, and it is the first condition for creativity and
experiencing" (185). Von Pierow cuts up several of his sculptures and moves on to his own personality with the same
violence. As the murder in the cave in the final section of *Cain's
Memoirs* signifies that Cain's life is smashed to bits, so he
too aims for a thoroughgoing transformation of his life. The cut-
ting edge of iconoclasm is primarily directed at the crippling
familiarity in which the protagonists are so firmly established.

Juvenilia begins relatively abruptly by telling about Torsten
Mannelin and ends even more abruptly with an anonymous
threatening letter. Not only are the three protagonists given
incomplete portraits, with their concrete similarities they also
tend to glide together in an enigmatic way; and in several parts
of the novel one can hardly tell who it is about. Nor do they
go through any kind of development toward a definite goal.
There is no very significant action. All of these devices lead to
the fact that it is even more difficult to read *Juvenilia* as an
ordinary realistic story than Gyllensten's earlier novels.

In order to understand *Juvenilia* one must instead concentrate
on the fact that Gyllensten wished to set up a play of roles
or masks. In the note in *BLM*, quoted earlier in this chapter,
Gyllensten declared that *Juvenilia* consists of "different literary
fragments, literary incarnations, which an anonymous author
(Cain) creates and puts together." But he also declared that
the anonymous author attempts to "shift incarnations, change
figures."[7] Mannelin, von Pierow, and Vickler are presented as
such shifting incarnations and figures. Behind them is the author
of the novel, and the three protagonists are roles or masks in
which he dresses. This implied author continues to be anonymous
in the sense that he does not speak outside of his roles, but
his book bears witness to the fact that he, too, is in Cain's
situation; and that is why Gyllensten can call him Cain in

parentheses. As roles, the puzzling similarities between the protagonists become comprehensible. They are not independent figures but can be referred back to one person, the anonymous author. The question is, however, whether Gyllensten did not also have Strindberg's dream-play technique in mind when he so consciously let the protagonists glide in and out of each other.

But as roles the differences between the three protagonists also receive special significance. One could say that they are expressions of different sides of the personality of the author and different attitudes of life which are possible for him. More than the others, Mannelin is dominated by impotent sympathy and the pessimism related to it. With his heavy melancholy he appears as the most tortured of the characters and the most cramped. Von Pierow incarnates more the possibility of rejecting that which is human. He stands in contrast to Mannelin's melancholy with a primitive vitality which at least partly receives its nourishment from vulgar carnal things. He also has a somewhat cynical trait. Vickler, too, is tortured by impotent sympathy, but at the same time he lives to a rather great extent in a rejection of the type which von Pierow seeks. In comparison with Mannelin's help for the retarded children he almost seems anti-social, and as an epileptic he is also close to what one might call a mystical sphere of experience. As a psychodrama *Juvenilia* thus presents evidence of tensions and conflicts in the personality of the author. The polemic which takes place between the characters of the novel may also be seen as an inner dialogue in which different attitudes are juxtaposed.

What is this psychodrama as a whole evidence of? One might characterize *Juvenilia* as primarily a novel of decampment. It is as if the collage method had given Gyllensten free room for action to establish his new situation after the end of his second period. By using the three protagonists as his roles he could pin down the most current questions for himself from different directions. In this sense *Juvenilia* almost seems to be an inventory of problems: problems are localized and formulated in order to be attacked later on. No solutions are given. With the exception of the anonymous threatening letter, it is Vickler's prayer for liberation from sympathy which concludes the novel; and the cramped situation remains throughout the book. Instead, *Juvenilia* incarnates a conscious and intensive attempt to break out.

It is also very obvious that the strategies presented in the novel are formulated with fumbling words. On this point as well, Gyllensten has made use of the possibilities of psycho-drama: with the help of his different roles he could formulate the different lines of action he felt he could see. Therefore, one finds no straightforward program, but rather a fruitful dis-cussion. But the different approaches made are nevertheless significant. They were to be continued in Gyllensten's subsequent novels, and in this respect *Juvenilia* is to a great extent a point of departure for the third period in his work.

This attitude of seeking in *Juvenilia* becomes perhaps espe-cially clear if one looks at the discussion on iconoclasm. There can hardly be any doubt that what iconoclasm is expected to lead to is given two different interpretations. First, and most important, iconoclasm is presented as a necessary precondition for new experiences and insights. One of von Pierow's formula-tions is representative:

In this way, by pressing the formulae and images and patterns as hard as one can, one finally makes them break, so that the senses, understanding, and art renew themselves, are expanded and find new nourishment—youth, to live, yes, by God: love. (214)

But the hope of attaining an insight beyond all human images and concepts is also linked to iconoclasm. As in *Cain's Memoirs*, it is a question of something which cannot be grasped with words, only guessed at. Vickler, especially, is close to such an insight. In the novel his epilepsy is called "the illness of the prophets and divine men" (116), and his seizures are described with a language borrowed from the mystics. In other words the possibility of experiencing the world and one's self in a new way is contrasted with a mystically colored insight into the innermost core of existence. The tension between these two ways of seeing things would recur in some of Gyllensten's subse-quent novels.

III   *Heaven or Hell*

The year after *Juvenilia* was published Gyllensten had already completed the short lyrical prose novel *Lotus in Hades*, and it is a direct continuation of one of the two main themes in *Juvenilia*: the possibility of rejecting the world. In a very suggestive way it describes a state of liberation which appears seductively tempting. Gyllensten chose a few lines from Baudelaire's well-known poem "L'Invitation au voyage" as a motto for the novel. In dark glowing words this poem paints a picture of a place of respite away from hard reality, a refuge that has some of the characteristics of an exotic island but which can also be interpreted as a state of existence after death. The lines Gyllensten quotes describe the happiness which exists in this distant place: "Lá, tout n'est qu'ordre et beauté, / Luxe, calme et volupté."[8] And this attraction to an almost absolute state of happiness also recurs in Gyllensten's novel. But further on in *Lotus in Hades* Gyllensten opens up a critical perspective as well. In *Juvenilia* von Pierow speaks of the bestial and paradisical freedom which exists outside of humanity and adds: "In Gethsemane" (167). It was in Gethsemane that Judas betrayed Jesus, and von Pierow's reflection probably signifies a reminder. Perhaps the freedom he wishes to attain is in actuality a betrayal of the people around him? In the same way, in *Lotus in Hades* the question is whether the euphoric liberation the novel describes is perhaps a blind and irresponsible state. This profound ambiguity remains throughout the novel.

Both abstractly and concretely, the framework of *Lotus in Hades* is given in the title. Hades is, of course, the kingdom of the dead of classical mythology, and it is there the novel takes place. The people acting in the novel are dead and appear as shadows of the people they once were. One notes among them several well-known Greek mythological figures: Odysseus, Tiresias, Hector, and Jocasta. But in everything else Gyllensten has proceeded anachronistically. In his Hades there are not only biblical figures like Cain and Lot, but also literary figures from later times—like Don Juan and Romeo, for example. He breaks through the framework of time even more violently when he includes a few contemporary Swedes. But the shadowy existence in Hades still appears throughout as an image for the mental state the novel wishes to capture, and the lotus fruit with its ability to make one forget has just as important a function. What is characteristic for Gyllensten's Hades is the fact that all of the shadows there have been almost completely liberated from the memories of what once happened to them in life. It is above all the ability to forget which makes Hades into a kingdom of happiness.

However, the intense suggestiveness which emanates from *Lotus in Hades* is primarily created by the use of a more concrete narrative technique. In the eleventh song of the *Odyssey*, Odysseus makes the journey to Hades by sea. He makes a blood sacrifice, and the souls of the dead come in a stream toward him. A few of them come closer and he is allowed to speak with them—among others his mother, Achilles, and Tiresias. But after they have finished speaking with him the dead return to the subterranean sphere. In a similar way Gyllensten allows the shadows in his Hades to meet the reader, speak for a short while, and then once again disappear. The shadows themselves describe what it is like in Hades, and it is they who praise the life there. In some parts of the book the author even asks them questions which they answer. They also tell about their lives, and sometimes they make trips to the world of the living. This narrative technique is not, however, used consistently; and there are several paragraphs, especially near the end of the novel, which do not feel as if they were spoken. This is true, for example, of four sections which develop some of the ideas of the Swedish religious philosopher Emanuel Swedenborg.[9] Swedenborg's presence in *Lotus in Hades* indicates the central role he would come to take in Gyllensten's subsequent novels.

The very first shadow the reader meets has important information about life in Hades. He remembers that he had his own name when he was a human being. But he no longer asks how the name sounded and characteristically enough, he remains anonymous. He declares that among people, each one watched over his own things and each was very careful to distinguish himself from the others. But as shadows in Hades people are empty and thin and glide into each other. His memories lie in ruins and decay more and more. Nor does he remember any goal outside of himself. Inside things pale as with the approach of dawn, and he is moving toward an almost complete disintegration of his identity. But in return the bits of his memory which remain fill him completely. The least little crumb gives him enough; and therefore he lives in abundance, rich as a troll.

This state of dissolution is described more closely by the following shadows. Odysseus explains that during the siege of Troy he was included in a fellowship with equals, superiors, orders, and responsibility. Now there is no longer anyone who has command over him, and he lives among the remains of what once was. He remembers the horse which became his greatest stratagem of war. The inside was also shaped like a horse, and it was tight for the warriors who lay there. Furthermore, those who lay in the hindquarters had the others' feet to struggle with, and many of them were shod with horseshoes:

That is all I remember: the rank breath in the guts of the idol, the black darkness and the unusually hard edge of a horseshoe pressed against the cheek. (50)

This pattern is recurrent. Another anonymous man vaguely remembers a woman who died. It was probably not his mother but his wife—in any case he mourned her deeply and for a long time. But this memory is pushed away by the vision of a desk which he once owned: the autumn sun from the window makes a glass ball on the desk draw a complicated body of yellow-green light on a letter (30 cont.). In the same way Cain's memory of the fratricide has been almost completely erased. In a scene which is linked to the concluding fragment of *Cain's Memoirs* he remembers a dead body at his feet. He holds an object in his hand—perhaps an ax or a hoe. He does not know who the dead man is, but he guesses that it is someone who has been close to him. He no longer feels any bitterness nor any tenderness either. The only thing he remembers with certainty is that one half of the face of the dead man gleamed at him "with a transparent fragility like a cameo of jade" (28).

In other words, the shadows in Gyllensten's Hades have been liberated from that which was painful in their lives. To be sure, the painful experiences are only hinted at, and the reader must fill in the contours himself. But they nevertheless comprise the dark background against which liberation is drawn. What is actually in question is a devastating war which took a good many years of Odysseus's adult life, the loss of a beloved woman, and a tearing conflict between brothers. "Liberation from pain, liberation from love, liberation from force, liberation from suffering, liberation from fear"—this is the conclusion in more general terms (18). It is not possible to understand this longing for liberation if one does not fully comprehend the pain from which it springs.

But life in Gyllensten's Hades is not only liberation from that which is painful. The fragmentary memories which Cain and the man with the dead wife retain have an unusual brilliance, and in the same way the other shadows allow themselves to be filled with memories rich in pleasure. Romeo no longer remembers the bloody sword fights, the fateful misunderstandings between him and Juliet, or their all-too-early death. But the memory of Juliet's kiss has him completely captivated, partly because she left her eyes somewhat open in order to spy on the seriousness of his kiss and to enjoy his enjoyment, partly because a bit of one of her front teeth broke off once on a bit of gravel in a cup of wild strawberries, and he felt it like a little knife sticking against his own tongue: "I remember that, everything, everything! But everything was only: the sharp diamond which was set in her tooth, the black greedy look under her curved eyelashes. O Holy Virgin, how delicious she was!" (33).

However, the figure Gyllensten especially permits to incarnate this lust-filled surrender is Don Juan. In one of the paragraphs of the book Don Juan declares that it was not pleasure alone that drove him constantly to new women. In that case he would have been able to have married and always remained faithful to the same woman. Nor was it pride in owning them. That would only have been adding numbers to a collection. No, what drove him was the desire to be captivated and seduced himself. For him seduction was dizzying and intoxicating. It was a question of such an intense and total experience that the past was erased and all duties to the future were dissolved. Seduction is heavenly in "an all-encompassing now" (80). It is obvious here that Gyllensten is linking his story to Kierkegaard's interpretation of Don Juan in the first part of *Either—Or* as a person who allows himself to be completely captivated by enjoyment for the moment. In general one can probably see *Lotus in Hades* as a variation of Kierkegaard's aesthetic stages rephrased in Gyllensten's own terms.

The critical perspective in *Lotus in Hades* develops almost unnoticeably. It is partly established by the fact that the praise of the heavenly state in Hades is carried so far that the reader begins to be suspicious. The terms used to describe happiness also become more and more dubious and wily. In one place a couple making love are described as the beast with two backs. When they embrace each other they literally turn their backs on the world. They have no eyes on their backs, no ears, no mouths, and they do not see, hear, or speak. Sunk in each other they forget the tasks of the world and do not worry about the future: "The beast with two backs: two gratings around a closed and undisturbed garden of Eden" (43). By and by their heavenly preoccupation hints at simple ecapism.

But criticism is also formulated in more explicit terms. A collection for the suffering in the third world is described in very ironic words. The contrast between the inconceivable need in many developing countries and the small amounts of money given is glaring, and with a travesty of the well-known Bible story the givers are characterized as merciful Sybarites. The perspective is expanded as ruthlessly in a section which presents Europe as a growth on Asia: a brittle and fragile glass veranda, where people drink punch and eat hazel nuts with silver spoons. The luxury Baudelaire's poem speaks of has become the material wealth of the Western world which functions as the lotus-flower of our times. Shutting out the third world is nothing other than a blindness which prepares the way for a future catastrophe.

In spite of its modest size, *Lotus in Hades* is a remarkably complex novel. Life in Hades appears at the same time as a longed-for liberation from a cruel world and a shadowy existence alongside of reality. The lotus fruit both liberates from painful experiences and shuts out the realities which it is necessary to register. In one place the question is asked pointedly: "Is this hell or the home of the saved?" (100). And it is characteristic of the novel that this question cannot be answered simply. Sometimes life in Gyllensten's Hades really is a heavenly state, and sometimes it is just as clearly a sterile and irresponsible state. The presentation always shifts between these two perspectives, and in this way the ambiguity goes to the core of the novel.

But if one keeps the connection between *Juvenilia* and *Lotus in Hades* in mind then the interpretation can be taken one step further. The critical perspective in the novel means that Gyllensten is not seeking any kind of total forgetfulness. A total denial of the world would mean landing in a destructive emptiness and nonreality. On the contrary, violence and suffering in the world are realities which we neither can nor ought to turn away from. But the heavenly state in Hades can instead be seen as an inner place of respite of the type referred to by the protagonists of *Juvenilia*: a hole or cave in one's personality, where the voices and claims of the world do not reach. One can retire to this place of respite temporarily in order to find rest and pleasure, and it is also clear that Gyllensten sees this liberated state as productive in the sense that it can liberate new creativity and new possibilities for life. In *Lotus in Hades* there are seductive voices which express the temptation to turn one's back completely on the world. But in the end it is a question of a form of liberation which will give us courage and strength to live in the world.

As a description of one such inner refuge, *Lotus in Hades* can be regarded as a direct reply to Vickler's desperate prayer for liberation in *Juvenilia*, and it is a solution which seems completely consistent. But in his following novels Gyllensten would describe these problems in darker terms and seek a solution along other lines. Perhaps in the end the attitude in *Lotus in Hades* still means a cleft between the outer world and the inner refuge which revealed itself to be untenable in the long run.

CHAPTER 5

A New Attitude Toward Life

THE collage novels, *Cain's Memoirs* and *Juvenilia*, were a definite decampment. Gyllensten's subsequent novels are also collages in the sense that they are constructed with more or less clearly distinguishable texts or blocks of text.[1] But the fragmentary form in *Juvenilia* did not recur. In *Diarium Spirituale* the texts consist of the diary entries of a single person, and they express a definite line of development. *The Palace in the Park* is built up with relatively large blocks of text which consist of a man's memories from his youth. These memories do not come in chronological order, but they have an inner logic which makes their presentation feel like one great narrative sweep. *Man, Animals, All of Nature* mixes essay and narrative texts, which are tied together by the fact that the tone is almost always the same. The middle part of *The Cave in the Desert* blends different types of texts together as in *Juvenilia*, but the other two parts consist of continuous narratives. *In the Shadow of Don Juan*, finally, consists of one long narrative. In other words, the development through which the collage form went during the third period of Gyllensten's work meant that the collages at once came to consist of more similar texts and to a much greater degree were built up into solid and harmonious units.

This development of the collage form corresponds, however, to a change in Gyllensten's goal for the collage. In *Cain's Memoirs* and *Juvenilia*, the collage is intimately connected to iconoclasm and has a tearing-down function. The collage served Gyllensten as a means of freeing himself from the ironic narrative attitude in the novels from the second period and the positions he had adopted in them. But after *Cain's Memoirs* and *Juvenilia* he was clearly free to move in new directions and in the following collage novels iconoclasm is therefore no

131

longer a pressing issue. Instead, the collage form in these novels is characterized by a basic attitude of constructiveness and seeking. In the future, the method of constructing novels with texts became Gyllensten's means of finding new relationships and connections. It is as though he thought that in the actual process of putting his texts together he could in some way grasp the basic patterns and structures which influence our lives. After the demolition of the collage period, it was now time for intensive construction work on a new foundation.

Gyllensten found an important tool for this work in the ancient religious myths. An interest in mythical material runs throughout the whole of his work, and there are references to mythical figures in most of his novels. In both *Cain's Memoirs* and *Juvenilia*, the biblical Cain has a dominant position. But there can hardly be any doubt that myths in the subsequent collage novels received a more profound significance for Gyllensten as instruments for structuring and interpreting reality. He published a fake interview in connection with the publication of *The Palace in the Park*, which turned into a declaration of policy. There he declared that his novel is based on the myth of Orpheus and claimed that this myth constantly turns up in new versions in different times. This, he continued, is because myths have special and very important characteristics:

The myths' ability to stay alive and to transform bears witness to the fact that they express the basic vital conditions for the existence of human beings. I do not wish to call them archetypes in Jung's sense of the word—that smells too much of German quasi-religion. They are rather original and primal tools—counterparts to the wheel, the hammer, and the sickle—tools of culture, formers of culture, constantly turning up with new modifications, viable, fruitful, inevitable.[2]

This view of myths is carefully balanced. First and foremost, Gyllensten claims that myths have the ability in many senses "to profoundly grasp recurrent, yes, timeless essentials which each period then expresses on the surface according to its fashion." But at the same time he is anxious to claim that this timelessness of the myths does not mean that they exist outside of history: "One only has to reflect the least bit on those myths which have existed and functioned in the world and in history, to discover that the myth has completely different effects— challenging, awakening awareness, socially structuring, emo- tionally captivating, providing material, innovation, etc." It is these double characteristics which make the myths so valuable, and the program Gyllensten formulates deals with his wish to work with "myths as basic patterns" for his books.[3] The shift in direction this aim signifies in Gyllensten's work may be described in the following way: On the one hand it is clear that Gyllensten sought out myths in order to be able to grasp the basic conditions in our lives with their help. But on the other hand, just for this reason, the myths could also serve him as instruments with which to orient himself in his own times.

I *Death and Renewal*

Three years after *Juvenilia*, Gyllensten himself provided a suggestive description of the development his collage novels went through in *Diarium Spirituale*, which was subtitled "A Novel about a Voice." There is only one single character in the book, and he is an author. This author is not, however, described from the outside by a narrator; instead the novel consists solely of his working notes. What is more, the author long remains anonymous, and it is in this sense that he is only a voice. But for a reader who is familiar with Gyllensten's work, it is soon clear that the author bears Gyllensten's own character- istics, and things are clarified toward the end of the novel. In the very last chapter Gyllensten openly declares that he has constructed *Diarium Spirituale* on the basis of his own working notes. In his work with the novel he has played two roles: to begin with he is the author of the novel's working notes, but he is also, as the publisher of the said documents, the editor of the material. With a reference to the psychologist's method of letting children project their problems through play in a sand- box, he formulates his working method in the following way:

Working program for "Diarum Spirituale": first gather together the blocks in the sand-box, "the author's" contribution, and then build and experiment with them, let "the publisher" arrange the land- scaping of the sand-box. The method, the violence, the cane. (173)

This working program does not mean that one can simply set a sign of equality between the author in *Diarium Spirituale* and Gyllensten himself. Even if Gyllensten made use of his own working notes, he could have placed a pattern on this material which was not at all taken from his own life as an author. But that is probably not the case. The development through which the author in *Diarium Spirituale* goes so clearly corresponds to the process of reorientation Gyllensten himself went through during the collage period that one can read the novel as his own interpretation of the new direction of his work. Actually, *Diarium Spirituale* was almost certainly an attempt, for his own sake and for the sake of his readers, at establishing and clarifying his new goals; and the novel is therefore a very important source for the understanding of his latest novels. *Diarium Spirituale* especially provides a valuable insight into the way Gyllensten worked during the collage period. One could say that the novel is simply a demonstration of how his collage method functions.

To begin with, the author's working notes appear to be disconnected and difficult to grasp. He makes attempts at establishing positions, comments on his earlier books, tests ideas and suggestions by means of theoretical reasoning, and tries to determine a line for the continuation of his writing. The notes also contain sketches of stories which he carries out in order to test their possibilities and ability to stay afloat—he calls them "story seeds." A few of these sketches deal with the characters in *Juvenilia* and several of them take up themes which would recur in Gyllensten's subsequent novels. One could say that the working notes in *Diarium Spirituale* bear witness to an author in search of his next book.

Nevertheless, the disconnected notes fairly soon move in a definite direction. In chapter XXV, the myth of the Babylonian goddess of love, Ishtar, and her descent into the kingdom of the dead, is retold in a poem several pages long. As the author himself says in the following chapter, this myth is one of many which deals with resurrection: the goddess descends into the kingdom of death, has her insignia and drapings taken from her, but is given the food and water of life on the command of the father of the gods and men, arises from the dead, and leaves the kingdom of darkness. The lyrical form alone makes this poem stand apart from the working notes, but it also has a very significant function in the novel. The poem comes in about a third of the way through the novel; and when the reader continues with the working notes, it turns out that there is a similarity between Ishtar and the author. The notes reveal that the author is going through a development which corresponds to the goddess's journey to the kingdom of the dead: Ishtar's death and resurrection correspond to a state of improductivity in the author, which gives way to a rebirth in new creativity. For a long time the poem about Ishtar predicts the author's development. But on the last pages of the novel, when the author definitely arrives at his new book, the myth of Ishtar appears as the pattern for his own development. The novel describes, one could say, how the author spiritually makes the same journey as Ishtar the goddess.

When the myth of Ishtar is placed beside the author's working notes, his development becomes clear; and the similarity between the author and Ishtar is also emphasized by the fact that the author's language is linked to the myth. The author sees his improductivity as a state of spiritual death and the conquering of improductivity as new life. The working notes express and demonstrate this line of development. In chapter V the author states that nothing lives for him, and in a mood of self-pity he lists a whole catalogue of difficulties and pains:

I am slothful, indolent, listless, apathetic, all autumn: acedia, asthenia, hypochondria, apathy, idiocy, *pavor nocturnus*, insomnia, no appetite, tired of life, afraid of death, irritation, vegetation, agitation, depression. (13)

One of the key words in the author's description of the state he is in is "spleen," which for him means absence of life. In chapter XI he presents an analysis of the nature of spleen and states among other things, "spleen: what is spleen if not just that state which makes hell hell, that atmosphere which transforms a landscape into death's abode, that trait which characterizes living death, shadow existence?" (21). Nor do things live for him as he writes. In chapter VII he can find no reason

for working with his new book; and a few pages later he writes
laconically, "Nothing worthwhile done in almost half a year"
(36). Instead his language degenerates, and he begins to be
persecuted by meaningless and obscene rhymed verses. In this
painful situation the author continuously compares himself to
Cain: in the same way that Cain lived as a dumb animal in
the forest for a time after the fratricide, the author has landed
in abject poverty after his breakaway from his earlier positions.
In general, *Diarium Spirituale*, in its introduction, openly and
directly links up with the problems in *Cain's Memoirs* and
Juvenilia. As Cain was the central figure in the introductory
phase of the collage period, the development in *Diarium Spirituale*
also begins under the sign of Cain.

In chapter XXXV, however, a shift can be surmised: "Time
to begin writing something" (57). This turn pertains to more
than the author's search for a subject for his next book, and it
does not happen by accident. His notes bear witness to the
fact that he is also working on a theoretical level: in the destitution which has hit him he seeks ideas in different directions
which can be fruitful and challenging to him. With Emanuel
Swedenborg he finally finds an author who stirs his interest and
who eventually seems to be able to serve as an example for
his own attempts. This meeting sparks something in him: "It
almost feels like a hint of a budding enthusiasm, just now" (64).
He begins to work more and more consciously with Swedenborg's religious interpretation of reality, and by reading Linnaeus
and Strindberg he also follows up his ideas in Swedish literature.
At the same time the myth of Orpheus becomes important to
him, and he attempts to approach Orpheus's song for Eurydice
in the kingdom of the dead with different interpretations.

This continuous work in the spirit of Swedenborg eventually
bears fruit in the author's search for his new book. He is still
unsure and experiments with several different projects—his notes
overflow with question marks. But his search is now constructive
in a totally different way; and among the projects he sketches,
one receives a more solid form. As early as chapter V he played
with the idea of using his diaries for a literary purpose. In
chapter XLIII he has Swedenborg's *Diarium Spirituale* as one
of several suggestions for a title for a work consisting of fictive

diary entries in a borderland between documentary and fiction. In the last third of *Diarium Spirituale*, the idea recurs that in his working notes he has the book he is seeking as a *leit-motif*. "Once again the suggestion: this work-book is the song of Orpheus that I am seeking..." (148). And it is with the decision to realize this project that *Diarium Spirituale* ends. In retrospect the author sees his working notes as the song of Orpheus which once again made reality alive for him, and in the final chapter he observes that from having been in Cain's situation he has developed into "a kind of Orpheus" (172). And thanks to the fact that he arrives at the book he searched for he also completes the development which was predicted in the poem about Ishtar. With a solid and clear plan for his book, the author—according to the design of the myth—definitely leaves impoverishment for new productivity and new life.

One of the archetypal patterns which Maud Bodkin investigates in *Archetypal Patterns in Poetry* is what she refers to as "the Rebirth Archetype." She finds a definite movement to be characteristic of this pattern:

Within the image-sequences examined the pattern appears of a movement, downward, or inward toward the earth's centre, or a cessation of movement—a physical change which, as we urge metaphor closer to the impalpable forces of life and soul, appears also as a transition toward severed relation with the outer world, and, it may be, toward disintegration and death. This element in the pattern is balanced by a movement upward and outward—an expansion or outburst of activity, a transition toward reintegration and life—renewal.[4]

This description well captures the structure in the development through which the author in *Diarium Spirituale* goes—though for that sake one does not have to see his development as archetypal in Jung's sense. As the author himself emphasizes, there is such a movement in the myth of Ishtar: the goddess descends into the kingdom of death and after resurrection the journey moves upward again. And the language influenced by the myth in the working notes emphasizes the fact that the author goes through a similar development. In the analysis of the nature of spleen, spleen is directly linked to the kingdom of death; and in the author's discussion of the myth of Orpheus, Hades appears an an image of spiritual death. The element of movement appears especially clearly in the author's development in a few of the brief comments on each of the chapters of the novel, which Gyllensten collected at the end of the book under the title "On the Secrets of the Story." One chapter hardly halfway through the novel is commented on in the following way: "LIV. Insecurity, doubts as to the form—still in the kingdom of the dead" (177). And in the comment on a previous chapter the shift in the movement downward-upward is predicted: "XXV. Time to turn away from the descent, with will" (176).

In Gyllensten's interpretation, the myth of Ishtar with this downward-upward movement expresses the conditions for creativity. In the chapter following the poem about Ishtar the author comments, "The legend deals with the conditions of creativity—begetting and giving birth: renewal through annihilation, new life through the downfall of consumed life" (45). The element of annihilation is strongly emphasized in the poem where Ishtar's limbs struggle with diseases and her dead body hangs on a hook for three days and three nights. This process has its equivalence in the emptiness, insecurity, and anguish the author experiences in his destitution. Clearly there is also something painful and almost brutal in his annihilation. But for Gyllensten the significance of the myth lies in the fact that this annihilation is necessary and therefore good: the old and worn-out life must be destroyed so that the new can grow up. Annihilation is thus the price we must pay for each true renewal. In *Diarium Spirituale* an author goes through this process, but he is presented as an example with general applicability. In the comments which reveal the secrets of the story he is referred to several times as "Everyman"; and in an independent commentary Gyllensten claimed that the view of creativity which the novel presents is valid "whether one creates a work of art, a personality or a philosophy and a program of what one wants to do in life."[5] Thus the author's development is meant to illustrate the conditions which are valid for all creative activity and by so doing he also demonstrates the utility and value of the myth. In one of the first working notes sketching the plan for

Diarium Spirituale the process which takes place when the
author, in Ishtar's footsteps, arrives at new creativity, is described
in the following way: "Because it describes—no *is*—the condition
for love or creativity? Old stories become like new—no, are
revealed as new?" (46). In other words, the myth is shown to
hide an insight into the conditions for life which is still both
tenable and fruitful today.

What ideas, then, did Swedenborg have which would turn
out to be so productive for Gyllensten in his own work? What
fascinates him at first is Swedenborg's way of seeing divine
messages in seemingly completely inconsequential and even
vulgar events. The "horrid world" (66), as the author expresses
himself when he begins to deal seriously with Swedenborg, is
actually nothing less than a witness to the secrets of heaven. A
little further on the author observes in the same spirit that it
is a platitude that the world is as it is. But that the world
exists at all is a miracle, and for Swedenborg and his followers
the platitudes are sacred omens.

To Linnaeus: the antennae of a beetle, the fall of a serving girl
from the porch step call out God's presence with such volume that
he sees His shirttails flapping. To Swedenborg: in the dream the
vagina dentata converses with the voice of our Lord and passes
on a very personal, very worthwhile deliberation. To Strindberg:
the cloud in the morning farthest away over the street is a character,
the muscle beside women's knees, the smell of celery, the atomic
number reveal important messages. (88 cont.)

In the author's discussion about Swedenborg's way of decoding
the world of the senses there is also a more subjective interpretation. Fairly far along in *Diarium Spirituale* he wonders
whether the events he notices have a message for him because
he distinguishes just these events among everything which
happens around him in the world: "There is a world which is
mine, my reality where *I* have something to devote myself to"
(106). The underlying idea, which is developed in detail at the
end of the novel, is that our personalities are formed in an interplay with the reality around us. Therefore we will inevitably
come to correspond to reality, and it is via these correspondences
that the world becomes rich in meaning and significant for us.

But according to both of these interpretations, the task of one who wishes to work in the spirit of Swedenborg is to take notice of the messages of the world of the senses as consciously and intently as possible. The author formulates the task he feels he has found several times with increasing eagerness:

Listen with hallucinatory clearness, listen with a Linnaeus's or a Swedenborg's "naive" confidence—listen for the voice which is hidden in the world if the world wants you for anything, and listen with such eagerness as if everything in the world were the words of the voice and preaching its message, your task! (93)

Of course Gyllensten did not completely close ranks behind Swedenborg. He was captivated by Swedenborg's method of interpreting reality, and he uses Swedenborg's religious language to describe the method. But the religious reality which Swedenborg claims to reveal is alien to him, and characteristically enough he characterizes Swedenborg, Linnaeus, and Strindberg as a "Swedish line of madness" (72). Instead he reinterprets Swedenborg's method according to his own epistemological attitude and wishes to use it for secular purposes. This change becomes especially clear if one pays attention to his discussion of the Orpheus myth which practically corresponds to Swedenborg's ideas toward the end of *Diarium Spirituale*. In the author's final interpretation of the myth Orpheus becomes, in fact, the devoted interpreter of the hidden messages of the world. The song of Orpheus becomes the passionate interpretation to which he exposes reality and Eurydice corresponds to dead reality which will receive life once again through the song. Even though there is a mystical tone in a few of Gyllensten's subsequent novels, he hardly seeks another reality than that of the world of the senses. But his goal is still aimed high. In the end, Orpheus in *Diarium Spirituale* stands for an intensive attempt to find continuity and meaning in a seemingly chaotic and alien world.

Therefore, *Diarium Spirituale* does not end in any new philosophy of life or world philosophy, but in a new program for writing. It is especially important to emphasize that this program is a new venture on the part of Gyllensten. In a central chapter in *Diarium Spirituale* he observes, "Either the world wants nothing to do with me, and then I am living in exile, or else it does want to have something to do with me, and then it is up to me to answer" (93). These are the two hypotheses, and he cannot know with certainty which of them is the right one. But in that situation he chooses the hypothesis which appears fruitful and meaningful. There are no guarantees that he will succeed, but the venture to which the development in *Diarium Spirituale* leads signifies an attempt at once again coming to a meaningful interpretation of reality. After the defensive attitude in the ironic novels from the second period, this was an offensive program; and as Gyllensten himself points out in *Diarium Spirituale*, to a certain degree it meant linking up with *The Blue Ship*'s theme of "betting on the miracle" (94). Perhaps one could say that in the following novels he would once again tackle several of the problems which he strictly kept at a distance in the ironically narrative novels.

II *Seeking Reconciliation*

The Palace in the Park is a direct application of the program in *Diarium Spirituale*, but at the same time it is remarkably freely narrated. At first, the narrative technique Gyllensten uses feels tried and familiar. An elderly middle-aged man returns to an old villa on the edge of a small town in Sweden where he lived as a boy during a few school years. Then the villa was run as a rooming house for the school, but now it is only occupied by an old woman. She reluctantly lets the man in, shows him around the house, and finally agrees to let him spend the night in one of the many unoccupied bedrooms. The man apparently spends part of the day at a conference in town, but in the evening he returns to the villa and sneaks up the creaking staircase to his bedroom. The novel ends with him going to bed.

What is important about the course of events in the present is, however, that it constantly awakens the man's memory of the past; and these memories make up the main part of the novel. He consciously makes use of the old rooming house in order to make contact with the years of his boyhood and youth. The pictures in the living room are gone, but the faded patches on the wallpaper are enough to make him remember the pictures which once hung there, and in the same way seeing the empty and naked rooms of the house helps him to find the way back to his most profound and painful experiences. Almost everything that had to do with life in the old villa has been dead and gone for a long time. But in accordance with the interpretation of the myth of Orpheus in *Diarium Spirituale*, the man becomes an Orpheus figure, trying to sing the past into life again in his memory. This tension between the present and the past is of fundamental significance. About twenty pages into the novel the purpose of the man's memory process is clearly formulated as follows: "He courts his past and his dead. He seeks them in order to be reconciled with them, so that he will be able to live without guilt and to go rest..." (34).

Soon, however, it becomes evident that the construction of the novel is not one of a simple narrative framework around a number of clear memories. In the first place, the memory images glide into each other suggestively. Different environments, situations, and persons are so similar that it feels as if they recur in different images; and often the shifts from one memory to another take place via these similarities. Furthermore, a few important memories recur in different versions, a technique which gives them the character of a kind of rerun. Secondly, the boundaries between the course of events in the present and the memories are to a certain extent eliminated. As in *Senilia*, objects and experiences in the present reawaken memories in the manner of Proust, and in the process past and present mix with each other. A recurrent scene in the novel is the man sneaking into the house late at night, and a few times it is difficult to decide whether this happens in the present or in his memory. And certain parts of the events in the present also recur in the same kind of reruns as the memories. Time and time again the man walks up the gravel path toward the villa or sneaks into the sleeping house, and our normal concepts of reality are disintegrated in a dizzying way.

All of these shifts and retakes illustrate how the man works with his memories, and one could actually say that throughout the novel the narrative method reflects his process of remembering. The different versions of the same experience express the uncertainty he feels as to whether his memories actually tell him what really once happened, and characteristically he complains several times that he cannot really make contact with his dead. The shifts between the events in the present and the memories perhaps capture another side of the memory process: the images which come to him in the old house are so alive and intense that it seems to him that both of the time levels exist simultaneously in a compact moment. Furthermore, the effect of the shifts and retakes gives the events of the novel a dreamlike character. Both the events in the present and the memories are like our most forceful dreams: at once sharp and clear, and illusive and unreal. There can hardly be any doubt that Gyllensten used Strindberg's dream-play technique even more than in *Juvenilia*; and on the back cover (which he wrote) *The Palace in the Park* is openly called a dream-play in novel form.

But there is also another significant pattern for *The Palace in the Park*. Gyllensten has subtitled the novel "Rhetorical Portrait in the Manner of Giuseppe Arcimboldo," and the novel gives an interpretation of the latter's unusual paintings. Arcimboldo (1527–93) developed an allegorical art of portrait painting whose characteristic trait was that he composed the faces of the people portrayed with objects from their professions and occupations. According to the narrator's story, a gardener's face consists of turnips, radishes, kohlrabi, cucumbers, and leaves of lettuce; an adulterer's, of women's bottoms, girl's breasts, hips, thighs, and the bodies of naked women; a banker's, of florines, packs of bills, coins, and ducats, etc. The narrator surmises a very definite discovery at the core of this allegorical method: the keen-eyed painter had seen that people are marked and stamped by what they do. This remarkable art of portrait painting has apparently served as an example for Gyllensten in *The Palace in the Park*, and as far as one can see he regarded Arcimboldo as a representative of the constructive collage method which he adopted during the later phase of the collage period. One can say that in imitation of Arcimboldo he constructed a word-portrait of his protagonist by putting together the experiences which left their mark upon him, and like Arcimboldo, he seeks the connections between these experiences and the person the man became. In the end Gyllensten wishes to discover the meaning of the memories which make up the novel—the unity of past and present and the correspondences between internal and external life.

The old school rooming house occupies a central position in the man's memory. In the present the house is badly run down. When the man walks up the gravel path he sees plaster falling down, chipped paint, and empty windows with faded shades. The little glassed-in porch is empty of everything except a bare wooden table, and the door is nailed over with a masonite board. A run-down park surrounds the house. The gravel paths and flower beds have grown wild and the fruit trees are mossy and neglected. At the back edge of the park a river slowly flows past wild-grown tangles of alder and hazel shrubs. Inside the house it is even more deserted. The old woman lives almost entirely in the kitchen, and all of the other rooms are unoccupied. Most of the furniture is gone, and that which is left is covered with sheets. Everywhere the floors are covered with dust, rat droppings, and dead flies. Here and there patches of dampness announce a leaking roof. Everything bears witness to great desolation: once people lived here, but that was a long time ago. The description of the ruin is cast in dark, glowing words; and it is clear that the house has many symbolic functions. First and most important, the house probably corresponds to the man's feeling that the life he has lived is wasted and behind him. The desolation of the milieu has its equivalent in an inner desolation.

The school rooming house is not, however, the only important house in the novel. In the dream-play technique the rooming house often becomes in his memory the man's childhood home some miles outside of the city. This, too, is a big old wooden house with creaking stairs and windows looking out on the surrounding garden. It is not possible to establish definitely the concrete conditions of the man's life on several points, but he has probably remained in his home after his parents' death; and it is in this house that his own marriage is enacted. A third significant house is the city's mental hospital, where the man's mother was cared for during her last years of life. The large, almost palatial building does not glide together with the other two houses. But the mental hospital is also surrounded by a large park where the light night breeze sounds like deep breathing in the treetops.

The memories grouped around these three houses move in several directions and are not immediately connected to each other. The narrative method of the novel is such that the outer facts supplied about the man are relatively sparse, but some of them are important. According to the information given the man ought to be somewhat older than middle-aged in the present. Like Eric Vickler in *Juvenilia*, he supports himself by selling plastic articles, an activity which he basically despises. In general, the aura of desolation which surrounds Vickler recurs in him, and toward the end of the novel the relationship between them is underlined by the fact that the man's initials are given as E.V. (155). At the time of his return to the school rooming house his wife is apparently dead.

But through the experiences which are communicated by the man's memories his life nevertheless takes form for the reader. Several memories describe his gloomy existence in the rooming house during his boyhood, where one of the few things which brought happiness was a collection of pornographic books in a hidden bookcase. A few intense memories of his first experiences of carnal love jump out against this cloistered atmosphere. One summer day by chance he bumped into two women tenting beside a little pond. One of them was a mature woman who took him boldly. The other was a girl his own age, and under the surface there was an intense rivalry between her and the older woman—a constellation reminiscent of Torsten's relation to Gunhild and Ester in *Senilia*. The boy experienced intense erotic pleasure beyond all social and moral conventions together with the older woman, and he became violently disappointed when the two women suddenly were gone. Afterward he also felt that he had let the young woman down in some way, and this experience recurs in the novel. In another memory he waits alone in the rooming house for a girl from the town. But when she comes and calls for him he becomes totally strange and cool and does not answer her. Similarly, once while abroad he does not respond to a French girl's partly unconscious sexual signals to him, and she is deeply hurt. On one occasion he is characterized both bitterly and somewhat teasingly by the narrator as "the unreal offspring of a reserved, aged veterinarian and a shameful, beastly sick soap-bubble woman" (103).

The main theme of *The Palace in the Park* consists, however, of the man's memories of his parents' marriage and his own marriage. His father was a veterinarian, and in his son's memory he was constantly surrounded by the sharp smells of his profession. In spite of his big and powerful build, he had a remarkably gentle hand with the sick animals. Relatively well along in years, he married a young girl who seems almost unnaturally little and fragile beside him in their wedding picture. Her son mostly remembers her soft black hair, which flowed over her shoulders. His parents' marriage was, however, brief, and they had only one child. Soon the mother was struck by an indefinable uneasiness and anxiety which later intensified and became mental illness. Periods of anxiety and apathy were relieved only by brief moments of health; so to her son she became a bedridden invalid whose room one tiptoed past. For a long time his father took care of her himself, but in the end she had to be admitted to the town's mental hospital.

The son primarily remembers the quality of tenderness in his father's relationship to his sick wife. His father cared for her with the same gentle touch as he did his sick animals, and he did what he could for her. He also built side rails for her bed, which were put on during her uneasy periods. Once the son woke up during the night and saw his father walking around the yard in the moonlight with his mother in his arms to quiet her. But the situation was difficult for his father and long afterward the son understood that he had secret sexual contact with other women while his mother was still alive. For the son, his mother's illness meant that it was almost as if she were gone. Once during the night he sneaked down to her bedroom and peeked in through the half-open door. She slept calmly in the glow of the night light and he stood captivated by the sight of the white face framed by the black hair. But a moment later he was knocked over by a blow with a cane on the back of the knees by his father and accused of spying. Perhaps his father kept him away from his mother because of her illness, and this intensified his loss. The guilt feelings came later. During the years in the rooming house he lived in the fear that his mother would become so well that she could walk around the town and that he would run into her with some of his friends. In the end she died of tuberculosis; and as far as the son could understand, it was a way for the doctors to help the incurably mentally ill out of life.

The man's own marriage was no less complicated. Apparently his wife had an accident which made her a cripple. Her legs were badly mutilated, and she was bound to her bed and her wheelchair. She reacted to this fate with a fury and bitterness which became more and more self-destructive. She began to chain-smoke, and according to her husband this habit was basically a way of cremating herself in advance. In his memory she is constantly surrounded by a sharp cigarette odor, which forced itself upon him as soon as he came into the house and from which it was impossible to get away. Like his father he cared for her as well as he could, but eventually there was almost no contact between them. In her bitterness she turned away from him, and he could find no way to reach her. And like his father, he sought out occasional sexual relationships with other women. But in a scene which recurs several times his wife expresses her continued disappointment in him. Late at night he sneaks into the house so as not to wake her. It is completely quiet, but suddenly there is a terrible crash. He rushes into his wife's bedroom and finds that she with all her might has thrown her heavy crutch right into the mirror on the dresser by the foot of her bed. She screams and cries, but still avoids his eyes. All he can do is help her to sleep with sleeping pills and sweet port wine.

It is primarily the descriptions of these two marriages which glide together in *The Palace in the Park*. The old house, the mute woman in bed, the attacks of anguish, the half-open door into the bedroom, the side rails on the bed—everything from his father's marriage happens again in his. But still more important is that the emotional atmosphere is the same. As in *Juvenilia*, in both cases it is a question of experiences which are so difficult that they can hardly be endured—and even now, when the man reexperiences the scene with his wife's crutch in the present, it is so painful that he cringes and almost whimpers. Both the man and his father are faced with something irreparable and perhaps it is not the least the experience of the limits of their own power which is so difficult for them to endure. Yet neither of them can be free from feelings of inadequacy and guilt. Finally, the many similarities between the father and the son point in the direction of a very important insight: perhaps the man has been so profoundly marked by the experiences of his parents' marriage that he repeats the same pattern in his own marriage.

One must admit that in a way there is an even more somber tone of despair over the conditions of man in *The Palace in the Park* than in *Cain's Memoirs* and *Juvenilia*. In the comments which the narrator weaves around the man's memories, a profoundly pessimistic view of life is expressed. In the beginning of the novel the man observes that the lime-wood frame of the house is visible from behind the falling-down plaster and he thinks he sees a native hut peeping forth from behind the fancy façade. The narrator continues,

A play with masks is enchanting, it makes the imagination fly—but the flight is a flight in one place, the enchantment changes the sight but does not change the foundations and the basic conditions: death is just as certain now as ever before, adversity is his swift-footed bailiff and agent.(50)

Further on in the novel the same imagery recurs. "It happens for the best," his father said when his mother died. But the son took the comment as an ingratiating attempt at transforming death from a hard bailiff to a liberator, and the narrator comments, "What are such ancient, antiquated incantations other than impotent attempts at hiding the raw facts of death and suffering with a plaster made up of sugar-water so that it will be palatable when one has to swallow it anyway!" (113 cont.). In these comments the crumbling house appears as an image for human life and the world.

But the question is whether it is not the intrusive experience of the human being's limited power which is the actual core of this pessimistic view. Even though we should like to believe otherwise, in fact we do not basically have control over our lives. The bitter realization that we are not sovereign gods but only demiurges who create on the basis of given conditions is a *leitmotif* throughout the novel. In general there is a strong polarization between the creative ability of the private individual and the forces of reality throughout *The Palace in the Park*. "He who competes with the forces which have created him shall be revealed to be an imitator and borrower, from whom shall be reclaimed all he has appropriated for himself," the narrator concludes toward the end of the novel (192). The tendons in our backs which hold us upright shall finally become undone so that we shall be bent and shall humble ourselves under conditions which are more powerful than we are. The works which are our pride shall in the long run reveal themselves to be perishable since they are erected on the foundations of the kingdom of death. Thus the interpretation of the myth of Orpheus related in *The Palace in the Park* deals less with the power of the song than with the superiority of death: in the end it is the kingdom of death which shows itself to be stronger than singing Orpheus.

Seen against this background, it is difficult to interpret the obscure ending with its many meanings in any other way than as a kind of capitulation on the part of the man. Throughout the whole of *The Palace in the Park* the run-down old house stands in contrast to the mildly murmuring park outside. Time and again, on all time levels, the man sits by an open window at night and thinks he hears deep breathing in the tops of the trees. The mild peace of the night is in contrast to the coercion and torture in the house, and he finally gives himself to the night. He sneaks up the stairs to the second floor one last time and goes to bed in the inhospitable bedroom. He takes sleeping pills, perhaps more than the amount prescribed. He has had enough, he cannot take any more, and he lets sleep or perhaps even death come. The last words of the novel are, "And then there was nothing more. The day has ended" (214).

But before this the man makes a significant discovery, which points in another direction. He does not know where it comes from, but it is at once both obvious and liberating. In a flash he suddenly sees the relationship between himself and his wife in a new way. It was not true that she was a prisoner in a cage while he was free on the outside:

Neither of them is on the outside and neither inside; they are both
caught on the wires of the cage, they vibrate with its strings, and
the one who acts, speaks, sings or plays is not the master of his
art but only serves as its tool. (210)

He has believed that he was free while she was the one who
was struck. But now he understands that they have both been
caught in a pattern over which they had no control. Liberation
is the result of the departure of the heavy guilt feelings. This
insight was prepared for earlier in the novel: "Who bore the
guilt? No one! It is the fault of the pattern, the game or the
antiphony" (148). But this liberation presupposes that the man
gives up his wishes to be godlike and truly accepts being a
human being with a human being's limited power. The narrator
states that life is not about sympathy, but participation. With a
smile the man gives himself to the night, but at the same time
his discovery points in the direction of a brighter and much
more life-oriented attitude.

III   *The Structures which Govern Us*

The Palace in the Park ends with the insight that our lives
are directed by patterns that we do not really see or manage.
Man, Animals, All of Nature may be characterized as Gyllensten's attempt at formulating this view on a theoretical level.
While it is true that the book contains a few fictive sections
which predict *The Cave in the Desert*, nevertheless by far the
greatest part of *Man, Animals, All of Nature* consists of short
essays and investigations which take up the ideas and research
results of a whole line of different scientists and philosophers.
First and foremost, Gyllensten refers to several expert ethologists
and there is no doubt that he was influenced by the blossoming
interest in ethology during the 1960's. Furthermore, he links
up with Chomsky's linguistic theories, G. H. Mead's social
psychological way of looking at things, and Charles Sanders
Peirce's epistemological ideas, among others. And he finally
even seeks out religious philosophers such as Augustine, Master
Eckhart and Pascal. This searching is emphasized as early as
the second section of the book: "*Collage* means the art of gluing—
one pastes what one can get ahold of ..." (13). But behind this

apparently disparate sample of thinkers lies Gyllensten's interest in the different types of patterns which influence us, and he continuously circles around these ideas. The book is also held together by a playful tone, which balances the high ambition of summarizing the results of research in so many different areas. Thus, for example, one of the sections which deals with the research of the ethologists begins in this way:

In the year 1910, Dr. O. Heinroth was wooed by orphaned goslings. He noticed that he was especially attractive to newly hatched baby geese, but not only to goslings, to new-born ducklings and water-rails as well. They gave him looks, if he was the first moving creature they caught sight of when they were hatched out of the egg—they followed after him, they were gripped by a mechanical and unreasonable devotion to him, as if he were their true father or tender mother. (52)

The discussion in *Man, Animals, All of Nature* begins with the animals and then goes on to human beings. In the first section, Gyllensten describes the experiments of Professors J. Y. Littvin and Humberto R. Maturana with frogs. They put electrodes on the nerve cells of the retina of the frog, then let them react to different shadows projected on a screen and in this way determined what the eye of a frog reported to the frog's brain. It turned out that different cells reacted to different signals. But most instructive was that a little round disk resembling the shadow of the insects the frog lives on made certain special and unusually vigorous cells send off showers of energetic electric impulses through the nerve up to the brain. However, if the disk was too large or too small there was no such reaction. The researchers drew the conclusion that the frog's eye is programmed in a very functional way: "The frog lives an interested life—it sees what it needs to see but nothing else; it only sees things which leave an important message" (12). In other words, there is a meaningful interplay between the frog and the world around it.

Gyllensten also finds this theory confirmed by the other ethologists and notices the importance they place on the training of the animal. For example, newly hatched chaffinches can cackle and peep from the moment they are hatched in the nest. But

before they can sing like full-feathered artists they must go
through a laborious apprenticeship of training and imitation.
There is a sensitive period during their growth during which
their innate talents must be developed, and the birds that are
prevented from listening to the trained masters during this period
never learn the art. An opportunity missed can never be made
up. Other experiments also indicate the same thing. Newborn
rats, apes, and cats who are forced to be alone in total darkness
a few weeks become stupid, aggressive, and homosexual. The
interplay with the surrounding world for which they have the
resources is never developed.

To a certain extent Gyllensten also applies this view to human
beings. He claims, in direct connection to the investigation on
the chaffinches, that there is no innate language, nor is there
any language which is only imitation. Instead he refers to Chomsky's thesis that there is an innate talent in a newborn human
being to create a language and that this talent must be cultivated
during the early years in an interplay with other human beings.
He also gives a line of examples which demonstrate that people
who were not allowed to take part in this interplay at the
right age never really learned to speak. Peter the Great, for
example, isolated some children in order to find out if they
would begin to speak the language of the Bible or some other
original language. But they did not speak at all, never got
further than jabbering and grunting. The significance of ethology,
according to Gyllensten, lies in the fact that it makes it very
clear to us that even human beings are to a great extent animals
who are steered by genetic codes and patterns, but that the
full maturing of the life patterns requires a constructive interplay
with social and cultural stimuli.

From this biological way of looking at things Gyllensten moves
up to an ideological level. Do we perhaps go through a social
formation of the same sort as the biological, he asks, and finds
a list of positive answers to that question. With Dr. George W.
Zopf, Jr., he reads that our sense organs are ideologically aware:
"How we survive and manage and how our interests are satisfied
determine what our senses and concepts allow us to comprehend" (21). He finds the same insight in Edward Sapir's linguistic observation that the actual world is to a great extent

built up of the group's linguistic habits and in Ernst Cassirer's thesis that the human being is so wrapped up in linguistic forms that he cannot see anything other than through this artificial medium. He seeks a theoretical explanation to this interplay between reality and language in G. H. Mead's analysis of how the human personality develops: "With the help of language one dons the roles which the other people in one's surroundings represent—and in this way one is formed by the attitudes which are predominant in the community" (167).

Purely theoretically, this view hardly differs from the epistemological positions Gyllensten adopted in the beginning of his career. But one could say that his attitude toward these basic epistemological conditions was transformed in a decisive way with *Man, Animals, All of Nature*. In *Diarium Spirituale*, he had already, as a disciple of Swedenborg, approached the thought that chaotic reality actually bore forth important messages, and he continued that line now by placing the interplay between the individual and reality in the center. To begin with he often touches on the idea that somewhere in the depths there should be a congeniality between the human being's attempts to win knowledge and the world that he is investigating. For example, he wonders along with Peirce, whether the human brain has a natural tendency to imagine true theories on reality (65).[6]

But still more important is that he more and more explicitly presents the extensive interplay going on between the individual and reality as a meaningful process. The world is still both good and evil, and the pronouncements on the nature of the world are many and perplexing. But because we human beings are formed in an interplay between ourselves and reality we can find meaning in this interplay and a value in our lives. This world in which we are born becomes our world and it is here we can be active. Perhaps one could say that it is basically a question of accepting the world in which one has landed, and characteristically enough this feeling of being at home is formulated in words which imitate Swedenborg's language:

What you do, you do—and what you say, you say. And you should be responsible for everything, for what you say is you and what you do is you. You are at home, wherever you turn. (154)

We can, of course, break this interplay by rejecting the world. That was Cain's way in *Cain's Memoirs* and *Juvenilia* and it is also a recurrent theme in *Man, Animals, All of Nature.* But now Gyllensten rejects this possibility: to break the interplay in which we are born is to go out into chaos and emptiness. "Despising people, anger—to turn away is easier than to serve" (193)—this is instead the insight arrived at in *Man, Animals, All of Nature,* and the words could be the motto for Gyllensten's next novel.

IV   *A Lesson in Humility*

The Cave in the Desert is one of Gyllensten's major efforts, and in several ways it became the final stone in the building which began with the constructive phase of his collage period. With breadth and force he gives form to the questions he had begun working with on a theoretical level in *Diarium Spirituale* and then developed further in *Man, Animals, All of Nature.* But he also reached directly back to *The Palace in the Park* and its milieus and characters. I believe that one could say that the new attitude toward which he had been moving in the previous books began to take a solid and clear form in *The Cave in the Desert,* and it is perhaps for this reason that the novel exhales a remarkable peace in spite of its somewhat somber tone.

The breadth of the novel is not the least due to the fact that it consists of three dissimilar parts which move in time from 200 A.D. to the contemporary period. In the first part Gyllensten relates the life story of the Saint Anthony to gain knowledge from it. He places great emphasis on the fact that Saint Anthony grew up at the time of the collapse of the Roman Empire. One emperor after another was crowned and killed, and the empire was attacked from the outside by Goths and Persians. Constant battle trains, taxes and debt collections, sponging soldiers, fires and plundering—everything was a tribulation. Furthermore, a whole line of different religious ideologies struggled for souls in a very confusing way. In this situation many saw a dark future and by using a modern term here and there Gyllensten points out that similar frames of mind exist today. In general, the heavy pessimism from *Cain's Memoirs, Juvenilia,* and *The Palace in the Park* is the point of departure for *The Cave in the Desert.* "One was born to live—bound to have things go badly—doomed to die—created unable to do much" (7), a characteristic phrasing from the first page of the story.

In Gyllensten's version Anthony is a young Egyptian farm boy who grows up in a well-to-do Christian home. After his parents' sudden death he takes over the family farm and manages it for a few years. But like Cain in the final fragment of *Cain's Memoirs*, he soon feels that he works in vain and sells the farm. His reaction to the collapse of the empire around him is to turn his back on the world, and step by step he moves further and further out into the desert. He first moves to the edge of the village and hardens his body with hunger and cold. But when people begin to come and admire his exercises he moves further out into the desert. He finally closes himself in an abandoned citadel, whose walls protect him from all human contacts. Totally alone he continues his exercises in mastering himself and attaining an inner emptiness which corresponds to the emptiness of the desert. He remains in his hole for twenty years.

But his exercises do not lead to the planned result. After a while it is as if the vacuum itself begins to talk to him. He does not think that it is so strange that thoughts of his sister and other relatives begin to attack him. He wonders whether he really was right in abandoning them, and he longs for them. But he is also visited by visions which he finds shabby and meaningless. Suddenly the clumps of earth on the floor are transformed into delicious looking loaves of bread, and his matted sheepskin becomes a puffy pillow. A woman comes out of the cracks of the stone wall with a wide open womb, and out of a corner crawls a naked boy with a wiggling bottom. He, who uses all his force to conquer himself, must experience the fact that his body is stronger than his will. The world he has rejected instead emerges from within.

But this is not all. A few monks live outside of the citadel, and they lift water and bread in a basket over the wall to Anthony. After a while, however, rumors are spread about the

hermit and people begin making pilgrimages to the citadel. Sick
people try to be cured by getting hold of some article that
he has touched. To appease them, the monks give Anthony a
new water jar every day and sell them later to people seeking
help. But soon the demand is so great that they must break
the jars and make amulets of the pieces. Within a few years a
new village has grown up outside of the citadel; and without
knowing it, the unworldly hermit is the reason for a whole
industry which exploits his holiness.

It is, however, this double defeat which is instructive in
Gyllensten's interpretation of Anthony's life story. In his story
Anthony does not resist victoriously the temptations to which
he is subjected; he must instead learn that it is not possible to
turn one's back on the world. He has attempted completely to
deny the world by attaining a state of total desolation both
inwardly and outwardly. But his experiences in the citadel force
him to see that as long as he lives he is part of the world with
his feelings and desires, and he cannot prevent other people
from using him for different worldly purposes. He struggles
against these insights for a long time. But in the end they are
decisive for him and once again, in stages, his path leads back
to the world. First he begins to speak with the monks over
the wall, and later he makes a habit of climbing over the wall
and sitting together with them in the afternoons. A little while
later he goes down to the village of monks and speaks with
the pilgrims. Toward the end of his life he even travels in to
Alexandria to protest against the Emperor Maximinus's cruel
persecution of the Christians.

It is obvious that Anthony goes through a very radical and
profound development in Gyllensten's story. His anger and
disappointment about the situation in the collapsing Roman
Empire lead him to turn his back on the world. It is a protest
which springs from realistic observations of the universal pain
of the human condition. But there is also a touch of arrogance
in this protest. Anthony's relationship to the world is to a rather
great extent a question of power. He cannot really bear the
fact that he cannot control the state of things in the world,
and the question is whether it is not in anger over this fact
that he turns his back on the despicable world. This struggle

for power becomes especially clear in his ascetic exercises. It is as if he sets his will against his body in a kind of cold fury to demonstrate that he is at least the master of his own body. And he also feels in the beginning that the visions which show that the body is stronger are insults and humiliations. Here is the same extreme polarization between the private individual and reality as in *The Palace in the Park*.

Thus, the insight to which Anthony comes that it is impossible to reject the world is to a great extent a lesson in humility. In his struggle for power with the world he must finally recognize that he is the loser. Even more important is that he is slowly able to accept these conditions. What happens to him in the citadel is that he gives up his furious claims to power and accepts the fact that the power which is actually his is the human being's very limited power. His main thought when he returns to the world is that he must do as well as he can. But he can never be completely sure that his actions are really just and correct. It is not for him to judge.

Thus Anthony's defeat in the citadel is a victory in the end. Although the humility he reaches tells him that he is more tied down than he could ever have guessed before, it finally grants him "a kind of liberation" (41). The monks note that he seems a bit more tied to humanity and, according to the narrator, his life after his stay in the citadel is characterized by "a calm cheerfulness" and "a secure peace" (51). He has finally accepted that he is "a created being who may be found where he has been placed" (45), and on the basis of this line of development he functions as a model in the following parts of *The Cave in the Desert*.

The second part consists of a great number of pieces of varying length and character. Several of them formulate and give form to feelings and reactions which lie behind the wish to reject the world. A suggestive expression of the total impotence we can experience as individuals is presented in one section. A man is on a train which passes a large residential area. By chance, in one of the many hundred windows he sees a man beating a woman: in a terrible and steady way he hits the already unconscious woman in the face time and again with his fists. But the man on the train can do nothing. The train charges on further and a second later the sight is gone. He does not have time to show any of the other passengers what is happening, nor does he even have time to localize the window on the huge façade of the house. Even had he used the emergency brake he would not have been able to point out the right window. What he has seen is clearly and obviously the crudest violence, but he is a powerless witness.

People's violence against each other and the cruelty of existence are in general a pervading theme in the second part. A Roman woman who is reminiscent of Elisa in *The Senator* appears in a few sections. Like Elisa she feels ensnared in the form of life which is offered to her, and she attempts to break through all limits with the help of sexuality: she devotes herself to a sado-masochistic game with a captured slave which the narrator compares to the bloody gladiatorial games. But Elisa's sober coming to her senses is in contrast to the terrible end the Roman woman meets. One morning she is found dead in the courtyard outside her bedroom with her head crushed against the stone floor. Without salves and rouges, her face is pale and etched with small wrinkles, and the gaping mouth reveals a broken and decayed front tooth. But the stiffened facial expression primarily bears witness to a bottomless horror and anguish. It is no longer a human being lying dead in the courtyard, the narrator writes, "but an incarnation of evil and pain and distress and affliction" (186). A more somber and intrusive image of the destructive forces of life and the superior powers of death is hardly possible.

However, the main thread of the second part of *The Cave in the Desert* is made up of a line of episodes dealing with a historical person connected with Anthony: Bishop Athanasius of Alexandria, who wrote the first description of the life of Anthony. He is introduced in a scene which at once is a sharp and revealing characterization of his personality. The old man, as he is called by the narrator, is in flight from Alexandria because of one of the innumerable intrigues which are raging around the Roman Empire. Disguised and riding on an ass, he makes his way through the night together with some of his faithful. At first he refused to put himself in safety, then he let wisdom speak; but he is furious that his own plans were disturbed and that he is forced to participate in this masquerade-like flight. He thinks about the celebrated occasion on which Jesus humbled himself by riding on an ass, but the thought gives him no real comfort. The road goes through the slum areas of the city and the muck on the streets stinks. Suddenly rats run across the road, the old man sees the cadaver of a dog, and a big rat stands up on its back legs and hisses at him. Now he has had enough and he lets his anger loose. He raises his fist against the sky and the sinewy arm trembles in bitterness. His voice is guarded, but from such a little body it is a surprisingly deep bass voice:

Stink and filth wherever you go! Living death wherever you look! The Lord of the world reigns over carrion! (61)

Athanasius knows that it is this anger which has been the driving force in his life; and even now, at the age of seventy, it makes him as hot as it did in his youth. It is anger which has made it possible for him to defy poverty and danger, ridicule, persecution, and even scorn. But he also knows that his anger is unusually complex. It is not only born out of indignation at the fact that truth and justice fare badly in the world. It also includes bitterness because he himself cannot immediately bring about change and improvement. The violent sympathy which is awakened in him at the sight of the toils of men throws him into as violent a feeling of impotence, and

The furious impotence hid a core of insatiable, unreasonable and profane or even bestial desire—fury because he himself was not the Creator and Lord. (67)

Here it is clear that Gyllensten forces the analysis of the desire for power which is dealt with in *The Cave in the Desert* a step further than in the first part. Anthony's anger and disappointment over the situation in the world shows itself in the figure of Athanasius to be nothing less than violent bitterness at not being omnipotent. The little old man, to be sure, preaches that the creations of man are not good for anything, but he cannot actually stand the fact that he cannot run the world as he would like to. In this way his anger is not only a completely irrational self-elevation. It also leads him astray by constructing unrealistic ideas of how we human beings can influence the world around us. Perhaps the old man's illusions of omnipotence are in fact the reason for his feelings of total impotence.

According to the pattern set in the story of Anthony, however, Bishop Athanasius must also learn a lesson in humility. He lives in exile throughout the book. And though he lives on a farm not far from Alexandria and is able to receive visits and send messengers, he is not happy away from the center of power and his very willfully directed activity. He begins to sleep badly and like Anthony he is attacked by memories and dreams. From a previous exile in Gaul clear memories from his meetings with the sexually possessed Roman woman and her brutal death arise completely inexplicably. But he is primarily disturbed by all of the animals on the farm. The frogs croaking, the roosters crowing, ducks quacking, and dogs barking force themselves upon him and keep him awake. The sounds become visitations, and he finally guesses that they have an important message for him: the animals remind him that even he, the powerful bishop, is a creature of creation who lives submerged in the stuff of the world.

This insight is driven even further into the obstinate old man by his meeting with an unusual fool, who is called Dog Chief by the people in the area. Surrounded by a pack of wild dogs, this fool comes to the farm in the company of a long-haired old goat. One of his tricks is urinating against his own cane while standing on all fours like a dog. At first Athanasius regards him only with repugnance, but they confront each other three times. The first time the Dog Chief gives a kind of performance for the people on the farm. Suddenly he puts his index fingers in his ears, turns his palms outward, places his thumbs over his eyes and yells out a verse in several variations: "Fingers in ears— so I hear better! Thumbs on the eyes—so I see better! Babble and howl like a fool—so I speak more clearly!" (163).

The verse is explained the second time the two meet. First the Dog Chief jestingly begs pardon because his dogs have disturbed the great bishop. But he then delivers a sermon on reason with a droning voice. How can Athanasius become angry at the howling animals, he asks. He closes his eyes and ears in anger and scorn. But how does he know that he is not hearing the voice of his Lord? According to the Dog Chief it is instead a question of listening correctly and seeing correctly and in this way understanding one's position in the world and finding one's purpose in life. It is especially important that the servant does not master the voice of the Lord nor judge the means the Lord utilizes.

The third meeting deals even more clearly with humility. The Bishop asks the Dog Chief whether he is baptized and is answered that he has taken not less than two baptisms. He received the first one when he was born and he calls that one the fool's baptism. But he took the second baptism when he became the Dog Chief, and by openly becoming a fool he actually left foolishness behind. With that baptism he made manifest the fact that he is "the servant of someone other than the emperor and the lords, the serving man to something other than his own glory" (205). As an ideal he refers to Marcus Aurelius, who saw that the power and glory of the emperor was only apparent and instead served the task his position implied. In other words, in their last confrontation it is the foolish Dog Chief who has the most profound insight while the temperamental bishop with his furious claims to power appears as something of a fool. But at the same time the meeting makes Athanasius interpret the message presented by the Dog Chief and he feels humility beginning to be born in him. Finally the Dog Chief gives him an old cape which Anthony had used until he died.

The last part of *The Cave in the Desert*, finally, describes a contemporary person who, in imitation of Anthony, lives a life in humility and service. Gyllensten has called the second part "The Spirits," and it is a title which leads one's thoughts back to Swedenborg: the reference is to the stories which follow, and they are spirits in the sense that they have intruded on the narrator with the force and clarity of dreams or visions. But Swedenborg's influence is even more apparent in the third part. In the spirit of Swedenborg, an older middle-aged man takes up the reconstruction of the life of Johannes Elfberg, accountant, dead for more than thirty years. The basis of this reconstruction is made up of the narrator's own childhood memories of Elfberg

and a much later study of the milieus in which Elfberg was
active. Behind this interest is the pedagogical motivation of
drawing knowledge from Elfberg's life. With a very "Sweden-
borgian" formulation the narrator notes that, "Every human
being we meet has, as we know, an instructive errand in our
own life" (222). Even the somewhat old-fashioned and sometimes pedantically ceremonial language is reminiscent of Swedenborg. It is also a verbal mimicry of an ascetic life.

Otherwise the action in the story is to a fairly great extent the
same as *The Palace in the Park*. The narrator in *The Cave in
the Desert* is not, to be sure, hunting after his own past, but
instead functions as a cool and objective observer. But in the
same manner as in the previous book, he returns to a house
where he has lived as a boy after many years; and the house
turns out to be the same school rooming house. This old house
becomes the image of a world which is threatened by ruin and
collapse even more clearly than the one in *The Palace in the
Park*. Furthermore, the narrator in *The Cave in the Desert* also
unexpectedly meets an old person who remains living in the
decay: a little old man who has made a large number of un-
finished figures of different sizes in molded plastic. The instructive errand which can be interpreted from the old man's
sculptures surely deals with man's strongly limited ability to
create: we are not gods who can create a world according
to our wishes; instead we must be satisfied working in the
world given to us. But more specifically, the old man is perhaps
also an image of the artist and of Gyllensten's view of his own
authorship as a series of different attempts at interpreting what
is finally a still unfathomable reality.

But the main character in the narrative is Johannes Elfberg,
and it is his life history which gradually takes form. According
to what the narrator can discover, Elfberg's relationship to his
father played an important role in his youth. When his father
went bankrupt and was socially degraded, his son stood by
him. No one knows what he really felt about his father's
humiliations, but outwardly he was unswervingly loyal to
him—here it is a question of the same problematic loyalty
which Torsten feels in relation to his blind father in *Senilia*.
He worked in the city bank for several years and after a while

his father's position improved. When his father died he inherited a small fortune and with the help of this money he carried out the only really significant action of his life. He, together with a midwife in the city, bought the house which is the center of the story, and they established a convalescent home which came to be primarily inhabited by incurably mentally ill people. When it became economically impossible to run the rest home, they instead transformed the house to a school rooming house; and it was here that the narrator met Elfberg as a boy.

The narrator places great importance on Elfberg's motives for his vitally decisive action. He claims that it was clear from the beginning that there was no economic profit in the project. Nor does anything indicate that Elfberg had an affair with the midwife. However, the narrator surmises that Elfberg went through certain decisive experiences during the years he helped with the bookkeeping of the city's mental hospital. To be sure, Elfberg himself never spoke of any especially unusual experiences, but the hospital must have sharpened his sensitivity for seeing how badly people can fare, his eyes having been opened by his father's fate: "The hospital was the place of the doomed—nothing happened there, no miracles could take place, no salvation was available to the imprisoned pensioners of the life which had taken them by violence for a shorter or longer time" (277). In any case, only a radical insight of this type can make the rest of Elfberg's life understandable, according to the narrator. In spite of unfavorable outer circumstances he toiled year after year to run the convalescent home, and it is this obstinate toil which is characteristic of him. He later took on the task of running the school rooming house just as perseveringly and indefatigably.

What, then, can this remarkable story teach us? To begin with, Elfberg's existence seems not only dull, but almost completely meaningless. All evidence reveals a poor and lonely bachelor life, and this bachelorhood becomes especially clear in the conscientious reconstruction of his room in the school rooming house. The large room, which was both office and bedroom, was barely furnished. The bulky desk was totally lacking in knick-knacks and the ceiling-high bookshelf held only carefully labeled cartons with bills and receipts. Elfberg spent a great deal of his free time in a high wicker chair with a thin cushion, drinking coffee and smoking thin cigarillos—according to the narrator he systematically starved himself. Beside the wicker chair stood a simple foot cushion with a band of oilcloth as protection against shoes. There was one single picture in the room, and it was of the children of some wealthy man in a little cart drawn by a pony. A naked light bulb hung from the ceiling under a white porcelain funnel. The sum of this description is that Elfberg to some extent appears as an ascetic hermit and his room as the hermit's lonely hole. Although he lived and worked in the school rooming house, his life has obvious similarities with Anthony's life in the desert.

But as the narrator gets further into his reconstruction, Elfberg appears more and more clearly as a heroic man. The action of furnishing a convalescent home was a totally decisive choice for his life. Once in his youth he made an inventory of the different possibilities open to him, chose the task which seemed to be most meaningful to him, and then remained unswervingly faithful to that task. As the narrator underlines time and again, he chose a servant's life in the sense that he totally and completely served the task he had chosen, and in this respect he also resembles Anthony after his sojourn in the desert. The increasingly greater economic difficulties in running the rest home, and the many practical duties with the old house—he took care of all of these jobs in patient obedience to the choice he had made once and for all. The attitude he represents must be characterized as strict discipline, and perhaps this strictness may partly be seen as a way of holding one's own against the temptation to turn one's back on the world. But apparently Elfberg's discipline had its root in a fierce passion which continued to burn in him.

In other words, the interpretation of Elfberg at which the narrator arrives is complex, and one could say that it summarizes the attitude Gyllensten finally worked out in his constructive collage novels. To begin with, Elfberg shows that man is both a stranger to and at home in the world. On the one hand there is a reclusive loneliness in his life, and there is no doubt that he denies and rejects the world in one way. The world is not his creation, nor is it created in the way he would like it to be.

In this sense man is unavoidably alienated from the world. But on the other hand, Elfberg is in another sense at home in the world he in part denies. No matter how it is, the world in which he was born and raised has become his world; and although he rejects the conditions in which people have to live, it is only in an interplay with his surroundings that he exists and can act. In this way the world has become just *his* world: "The poverty was *his*, and the toil was *his*, and the loneliness was *his—his* and no one else's. There he was at home" (260).

Furthermore, Elfberg presents as balanced a view of the power of human beings. On the one hand his servitude includes the insight that the lives of men are steered by forces which are stronger than they are. He cannot control death nor perhaps the fact that many people fare badly in life. Social patterns and structures can be transformed over a period of time, but we are often helpless in the face of their effects in the present. But on the other hand, human beings are not entirely powerless. The passion which lay behind Elfberg's rest home was, on the contrary, the will to help the ill and stricken. Stubbornly and untiringly he did what he could, and it is this endeavor which makes him a heroic person.

But through this Elfberg above all appears as a positive contrast to Anthony and Athanasius with their stormy claims to power. In his humility he is free from the illusions of omnipotence which possess them. Because of the dialectical movement of the novel, his serving and the limitations of his power are strongly emphasized. But what is most remarkable about Elfberg is still the fact that it is completely clear that it is a great liberation for him to accept his humanly limited power, and it is the same liberation which both Anthony and Athanasius experience further on in life. The unreasonable responsibility which accompanies illusions of omnipotence is gone as are the unrealistic feelings of guilt. Instead, he accepts the context in which he lives and finds a task for life which corresponds to his capacity. Instead of impotent attempts at being divine, he accepts that he is a man among human beings, and it is certainly from this acceptance that the remarkable peace in *The Cave in the Desert* springs most profoundly.

V   *Farewell to the Masters*

With Gyllensten's *In the Shadow of Don Juan*, it became even
clearer how much the constructive phase of the author's collage
period is a vehement coming to terms with a line of people
who passionately strive for power—or to use his own term,
"masters." According to the interpretation of the Don Juan
figure which he presents in his novel, Don Juan is not primarily a
man of sexuality, but a highly strung man of will whose whole
endeavor is to control himself and the world.[7] One might say
that in extreme exaggeration he incarnates the longing for a
divine power which, to an increasing degree, exists in the main
character in *The Palace in the Park* and in Anthony and Athanasius in *The Cave in the Desert*. Just through this exaggeration,
the lust for power appears in all clarity as dangerous and
destructive. Gyllensten's Don Juan radiates an intense fascination, but there is no doubt that he ends in terrible condemnation.
The hero of the novel is instead Don Juan's servant, Juanito, and
it is he who represents the new attitude at which Gyllensten
has arrived. There is high dialectic tension in the novel which
springs from Juanito's relationship to his master and the development of this relationship. At the end of the novel Juanito clearly
appears as a positive opposite to Don Juan.

In the Shadow of Don Juan is a novel narrated straightfor-
wardly, and it is obvious that Gyllensten has greatly enjoyed
retelling Don Juan's escapades in a long series of colorful and
vivid scenes. He has used the picaresque novel as a pattern:
Don Juan and Juanito are rogues, and his story has some of
the picaresque novel's episodic structure about it. Characteristic
of the first half of the novel is the alternation of separated sections
relating Don Juan's and Juanito's very different backgrounds.
Don Juan—or Master John, as Gyllensten most frequently refers
to him—grows up as a noble in a rich and powerful family in
Seville during Spain's period as a world power. His mother is
only a girl when he is born; she dies in childbirth, and her
son grows up as an only child in a totally masculine environment. The strict and authoritative father directs his son's upbringing from the very beginning according to the proud principles
maintained by the Spanish nobility. The young noble will one

day become the master of the family's widespread property, and he will also perhaps participate in the government of the country. Therefore, demands are made on him to "be great, as Spain herself is great" and "strong, as the Spanish nobles and seamen were strong." Greatness comes from strength, strength presupposes will, and will is born out of self-discipline (22 cont.). The point of everything is to be in control and to hold one's fate in one's own hands.

For a long time this upbringing runs its expected course. But during the years granted the young nobleman for sowing his wild oats before he enters into the adult world, something goes wrong. Master John sows his oats with a passion which exceeds everything previously beheld. He begins to get a reputation and is further incited to more and more bold and mad deeds of bravado. It is as though he consciously takes the traditional pranks and drives them to the point of becoming caricatures. His pride has grown so great that he even rejects the proud principles according to which he was raised. There is no longer any order to which he is willing to subject himself, and he really earns the name Master John.

This immeasurable lust for power is especially expressed in Master John's sexual conquests. It is not primarily because of desire that he seduces so many girls and women—in general he is far from being a sensual person in all his hardness. Instead the women he meets appear to him as challenges, and the many acts of seduction are primarily demonstrations of power. His victims are most often women who are happy or on their way toward happiness in life. It is as though he were provoked by their happiness, and his purpose is basically to defile them. He drives them to seduction with ice-cold calculation and then disappears immediately afterward. Behind him he not only leaves people whose lives have been ruined. Even more important is that he has had the opportunity to spit on the values and dreams on which they lived. Not only is he stronger than the women he seduces, but he also places himself above all ordinary human contexts and principles of order. Actually, he knows that he does not control the world: he is a human being and will die one day. But he challenges the world in furious defiance of this superior power. As long as Master John can move he is going to stay master. Perhaps there is still a possibility to feel strongest in this refusal to accept reality.

Juanito's background is completely different. He is the son of a kitchen maid in Master John's palace, and after a while he is automatically included in the staff of servants. There are no proud principles of education in his life nor any glamorous career awaiting him. He goes to no other school than the school of life; and this, for him, means "the life of the street, crowds of people, the bits which chance or fortune have placed in his way" (67). He roams the sun-hot streets of the city with his friends, stealing fruit at the market square, and fleeing over the many courtyard walls. Most things work themselves out as long as he is "quick enough on his feet, clever with his hands, sharp-sighted, smart-minded" (62). He lives for the moment, and it is a life with many detours.

In this "school" Juanito becomes another person than Master John. First of all, he has a softness which is in clear contrast to his master's icy hardness. The first time he experiences an adult's sexuality a strange mixture of uproar, expectation, joy, and uneasiness arises in him. Half in a dream he retreats and releases a few small birds he has captured: one by one he carefully throws them up in the air and watches them fly away (44 cont.). Shortly thereafter an older woman takes him to her and initiates him into erotic love, but after a while leaves him for fear of her husband. Juanito first experiences an intense joy in sexuality and then just as intense pain and loss. His softness means that he can accept what life gives him, but it also means that he is without protection in the face of things that hurt.

Furthermore, the conditions of Juanito's life make it impossible for him to fall into the illusion that he can control his own destiny. On the contrary, life to him is like a great and powerful sea. In lighter moments he feels he has an exciting and unfathomable adventure ahead of him. But he is just as often afraid of being at the mercy of such strong forces: "Life lived with him so that he often did not know what was up and what was down, right or wrong, wise or stupid, beautiful or ugly, or what he actually was" (63). The world seems threat-

ening to him, and he is afraid and unsure. He anxiously wonders
what will happen to him in his life.

It is just because of his fear that Juanito is attracted to Master
John. Even as a boy he was impressed by the taut figure on
horseback, and later he comes to admire Master John's superior
strength in his wild escapades. It is not exaggerating to suggest
that he is spellbound by Master John's proud and strong figure.
In him he sees a human being who is in control of every
situation without fear or confusion, and Juanito wants to be
like him in order to get rid of his fear. On one appropriate
occasion he helps Master John on his own initiative and as a
reward is allowed to become his servant. He follows him around
different parts of Europe during several adventurous years.

What happens during these years is, however, that Juanito
slowly glides away from his master. At first he enjoys being a
part of Master John's reckless escapades and adopts some of
the brilliance. But as time goes on he becomes more and more
upset over his rampages on the lives of others and sees himself
as a despicable accomplice. His laughter catches in his throat:
his master's roguish tricks are in reality nothing but brutal
aggressions against other people. Slowly his fascination with
Master John loosens its grip on him. Instead of a sovereign master
he begins to see an empty and almost dead human being. Behind
the brilliant façade he catches a glimpse of an appalling poverty
and despair. Gyllensten above all points out his profound loneliness: with his continually pale cheeks Master John is almost
outside of the circle of humanity.

The definite coming to terms takes place during the quickly
accelerating course of events of the last fifty pages of the
novel. In Naples Master John seduces a young, untouched girl
in what is even for him an unusually indecent and infamous
way. There is a scandal, the girl's powerful family demands
compensation, and Master John's father rejects him. Home again
in Seville, Master John is disinherited and forced to marry the
girl. The novel ends with him leaving Spain at his father's
command to supervise the family's trading company in the
West Indies. But even more important is the fact that his last
act of seduction ends in defeat. Before the scandal became
known his father had planned a marriage for him with the

young ambassador's daughter Anna Ulloa. In the belief that
she does not know about his forced marriage Master John acts
like her husband, climbing up to her window one night and
attempting to move her with his most glowing words of love.
But Doña Anna is not fooled and rejects him with scornful words:

Go home and go to bed Master Juan Tenorio! Your wife will surely
come soon. Have patience, only a few days, then the right person
will know how to clip your fiery wings! Have patience, Juan Tenorio—
another shall make you her tame goose! (203 cont.)

Through these events Juanito can finally definitely put his
master at a distance. He sees that Master John has gone too
far by his evil deed in Naples and been caught out by people
more powerful than himself. He is jubilant over the defeat
Doña Anna deals him—a woman has finally resisted Master
John! Actually, he himself has tried to warn Doña Anna and
shortly thereafter he abandons his master. In the end he sees
through Master John completely, and his own fascination for
him vanishes. It is not only that Master John's apparently
magnificent strength is an illusion. His furious lust for power
has also led him away from people and life into an appalling
emptiness. At the very end of the novel Juanito knows in the
marrow of his bones that his master's way will end in a state
similar to death:

Who is invulnerable—except one who is already dead? Who is hard—
except the one who cannot receive anything, the completely and
incurably poverty stricken? Who is strong and inconquerable—except
one who does not exist, one who is apart from everything and
everyone? (221)

But Juanito also has a positive insight to counteract the
temptation to play the master. In a similar way as the boy,
Abraham, in *The Blue Ship*, he musters the courage to accept
his littleness and his vulnerability. The world around him is
immensely greater than he is, and it acts with forces over which
he has no control. One cannot be rid of fear and uncertainty.
But he feels that it is nevertheless in this field of tension that he
is at home and able to find a meaning for his own life. Juanito,

in clear contrast to Master John's loneliness, stands facing his fellow men.

It is as though a long and difficult process in Gyllensten's writing comes to an end here. Juanito steps out from under Master John's lordly cape, and it feels like a definite farewell to masters on Gyllensten's part as well. Like Anthony in *The Cave in the Desert*, Juanito feels that it is good to be an ordinary person. It is a relief to be little! One last time he sees Master John on his way out to an awaiting ship and notes that it is good to see him disappear. Gyllensten says nothing about his fate. But on the last pages of the novel Juanito is recuperating in a hut by the sea. He has left his fine livery and sharp sword in Master John's palace and has "most of his pack and supplies in his bare hands" (222). Nevertheless, he is filled with peace and faces the future confidently. Thus, *In the Shadow of Don Juan* is a definite end point for the constructive phase of Gyllensten's collage period. But one may wonder if it is not at the same time the beginning of a new and exciting development in his work.

CHAPTER 6

Conclusion

I *The Novelist*

WITH *Madame Bovary* (1857), Gustave Flaubert established a new ideal for the novel which later went under the slogan-like name of "exit author." Many of the most significant novelists and short-story writers of the turn of the century followed a similar line, more or less in direct imitation of Flaubert: most of the Naturalists in France, Joseph Conrad and James Joyce in England, Henry James in the United States, and Chekhov in Russia. In the next generation the tradition was carried on by André Gide, Virginia Woolf, Ernest Hemingway, and William Faulkner, among many others. It is probably no exaggeration to say that the call of "exit author" influenced a great number of the novelists of the 1900's even up into the 1960's.

It is difficult actually to comprehend this ideal for the novel since in retrospect the ambitions brought forward by many of its representatives seem unclear and unreasonable. For example, what does an author "exiting" from a novel actually mean? In a figurative sense the significance is fairly clear: the narrator gives up his role as commentator and thus becomes less obviously visible. But when it is later claimed that the novel narrates itself or that the characters live their own lives—doesn't one then attempt to spirit away the author even as a physical person? These transitions create a peculiar feeling of dizziness, which may depend finally on a basic tendency to wish to erase the boundaries between the fictive world of the novel and reality.

However, the tradition of the novel emanating from Flaubert allows itself to be defined as a set of formal methods. The obvious point of departure for Flaubert, as for the realistic novelists of the first half of the 1800's, was to reproduce reality. But he had another way of accomplishing this reproduction. In

172

the first place he rejected the narrator's role as commentator and instead wished to adopt a strictly objective attitude toward his characters. In practice this meant that the essay-like expositions in which novelists before him excelled disappeared. In the second place he sought to substitute the author's narration with dramatic and graphic scenes to as great an extent as possible. The task of the novelist was not to "tell," but to "show." Thirdly, in this way Flaubert aimed to give the course of events of the novel as great an illusion of reality as possible. The author was not to be seen in his work so as not to disturb the spellbound reader's illusion of being directly confronted with reality. These new methods signified important new ground won for the novel. But as Wayne C. Booth has claimed in his critical analysis in *The Rhetoric of Fiction,* in the 1960's Flaubert's ideal of the novel came to be regarded more as a "crippling dogma."[1]

Flaubert's tradition came late to Sweden and did not make as great an impact as it did in the Anglo-Saxon countries. Strindberg's novels were influenced by the Naturalistic novelists, but he nevertheless maintained a solid base in an older narrative tradition thanks to his previous strong impression of Dickens. At the end of the 1920's Eyvind Johnson (1900–1975) experimented with an inner monologue in imitation of Joyce, but he later turned toward an open and ironic narrative position in his historical novels. It was during the 1940's that the tradition from Flaubert made a more notable breakthrough, and then the impulses came from the United States. Thorsten Jonsson, the critic (1910–50), analyzed Hemingway's and Faulkner's narrative methods in a series of noted essays; and he also attempted to use this knowledge in his own short stories: he used both a behavioristic narrative technique inspired by Hemingway and an advanced inner monologue like Faulkner's almost programmatically. And Hemingway's sparse and laconic narratives were also for a while the ideal of a group of authors called the "hard-boiled." Later, during the 1950's, a theoretical discussion of the narrator's role took place in the spirit of Flaubert.

However, there was strong resistance to Flaubert's tradition as early as during the 1940's. From the very beginning, Lars Ahlin repudiated illusionism in the art of writing novels, and Gyllensten's novels are just as clear a break from the ideal of

"exit author." As early as in the beginning of the 1950's he
wrote the following sharp reply to the discussion of the role
of the narrator:

I cannot see such discussions as, for example, the one of the point
of view of the writer, within or outside of the person described, as
anything else than issuing from a dogmatically limited pretense
on the art of illusion, in which the subjective projection in all
writing shall be censured by skillful maneuvering or by black-outs—
problems for illusionists.[2]

Later during the 1950's he directly returned to the tradition before
Flaubert by way of Thomas Mann, by openly playing a part
in his novels as an ironic narrator. And the collage method
he began to develop toward the end of the 1960's is even
further from the "exit author" ideal. One could say that Gyllensten's novels mean a significant expansion of the means of
expression of the novel in comparison to Flaubert's fairly narrow
ideal of the novel.

In his novels Gyllensten has especially developed a union of
intensely rendered scenes and essay-like texts, for which there
is no place in Flaubert's tradition. The role of the ironic narrator
in the novels from the 1950's is to illustrate, with his comments,
the events to which he gives form in the scenes and thus to
create a more profound understanding for that which is taking
place. The narrative and discursive parts of the collage novels
complement each other in just as artful a way. It is as though
Gyllensten needed the sharply rendered scenes just as much
as the philosophical discussion in order to encompass the experiences and insights with which he is working. This fruitful
tension between the almost "visionary" stories and the theoretical
analyses is one of the most characteristic traits of Gyllensten's
writing.

But even more important is the fact that Gyllensten's goals
for his writing are basically different from Flaubert's. With his
narrative methods he rejects the supposition that the novel
should reproduce reality or that it should create the illusion of
reality. Instead, his novels are openly and demonstratively arti-
facts, whose most important function lies in the fact that they
take a position in relation to reality. He does not hold up a

corner of reality for the spellbound reader; instead his novels are a means for him to orient himself in reality. Like Kierkegaard, in his novels he wishes to investigate the different ways open to us to relate to the world around us; and in this way his novels have significance for us.

II   *Surrender and Distance*

Gyllensten's dialectical writings comprise a whole in which the individual works at once argue against each other and complement each other. In a tangible and concrete way the works are tied to each other by a line of recurrent characters and motifs. As opposed to a traditional cycle of novels, there are no characters who are identical from one of his novels to another, and this point is made clear by the fact that similar characters do not bear the same name in several novels. Instead one finds different characters with similar traits and biographies. The outer similarities do not play a significant role—even though certain outer traits and conditions serve as marks of recognition. The important connections are in the ways the characters relate to reality and in the experiences they have behind them. They think and feel in a similar way, and in this way a definite atmosphere is created around them. In her dissertation, Kerstin Munck has accurately noted that Gyllensten step by step has built up a "theater supply of masks and marionettes,"[3] but at the same time it is not to be overlooked that the recurrent characters change all the time. Certain of his characters have clearly been especially fruitful for him: they have incarnated a complicated problem in such a way that he has been forced to work with them and to develop them from one novel to another. At the same time as he has plunged deeper into the problem, his perspective on the recurrent characters has changed. He has seen them in a new way, certain traits have been eliminated, others have emerged, and they have thus become different.

In the same way different works refer to each other through recurrent motifs, a technique which helps to weave together the individual novels into a whole. Certain conflicts, constellations of people and environments have also clearly been so meaningful to him that he has been forced to return to them again and again. But these recurrent motifs are not identical from one novel to another either. When motifs from previous novels recur, they are attacked from new points of departure and thus receive a somewhat different form. Both the recurrent characters and motifs are subordinated to a movement toward a broader and deeper understanding, which is characteristic of Gyllensten's work.

Seen more profoundly, the individual works comprising Gyllensten's total writing are, however, united by the fact that they move over the same problem area, and at the core of his authorship one finds a dialectical tension between *surrender* and *distance*. Gyllensten's novels express a view of reality which, it must be said, has a rather somber tone. To begin with, there is the insight that many people are tortured by the conditions in which they live. This is true for the conditions of life of the individual human being, which is often given an Existential emphasis. Death appears especially as a reality which is importunate and difficult to accept. But it is also valid on a collective level: in Gyllensten's novels history often is like a nightmarish chain of violence and suffering. This insight into the pain and misery of human beings is difficult to endure, and it stirs anger and sympathy in him; but it cannot be reasoned away. Furthermore, in many respects the world appears to be an absurd establishment. In his earlier novels, especially, the world was presented as a cacophony of noisy voices with no distinct meaning. Added to this world view is the recurrent experience that important truths are often interchanged with prejudices and illusions. This concept of reality may be seen in connection with growing Nazism and the terrible devastation of World War II (see Chapter 1). The point of departure for Gyllensten's authorship was a profoundly experienced crisis.

Gyllensten seeks to create a tenable and fruitful attitude to this world in his work, and it is possible to characterize one of the two poles around which he groups his attempts as a form of surrender to life. This surrender is put together in such a way that it looks like a Janus face. On the one hand it appears as a necessary and appropriate affirmation of life: an attempt at understanding what we meet in life and at acting in ways we find to be correct. It is a question of an intensive and active relationship to reality which makes existence alive and meaning-ful. On the other hand, there is something in this surrender which faces darkness and death. Attempts at finding a meaning in existence can lead to destructive impulses, and somewhere an attraction toward disintegration is also lying in wait. Sur-render thus has one face which is light and good, but also one which is dark and evil. And distance has a Janus face as well. On the one hand it includes the insight into the destructive forces which exist in life and the definite will to disclaim them. Furthermore, it means a critical or skeptical attitude toward reality and the many different ways of acting that are possible. On the other hand, the will to keep one's distance to reality can lead to too great a distance: distance threatens to turn into emptiness and sterility. Distance, in other words, also has its advantages and disadvantages.

In Gyllensten's work these forms of surrender and distance play against each other in different combinations. The good distance stands in contrast to the dark surrender, and the light surrender to the sterile distance. It is really a question of a contrast: sur-render and distance are forces which pull in different directions. The tension between them is often painful and difficult to resolve, and there is no simple solution in Gyllensten's novels. But at the same time one must be aware that it is also a question of a fruitful play of forces and perhaps one could therefore still say that Gyllensten's authorship points toward a "synthesis." It is not a synthesis of the type which cancels or completely resolves all conflicts, but a synthesis in which the two poles of the dialectical tension balance each other in a positive way. Surrender and distance move in opposite directions, but by being each other's correctives, they also complement each other. The synthesis Gyllensten's authorship indicates is there-fore an attitude in which the tension between surrender and distance is nevertheless fruitful. A section out of *The Cave in the Desert* captures this interplay better, perhaps, than any other single passage in his writing. First, he presents an image which is then interpreted:

The drop of water holds itself hanging in the hollow of the red hot iron burner of the wood-burning stove by surrounding itself with a shell of compressed steam. The shell protects the drop of water from immediately becoming gas. The drop boils hard on the outside of its surface. It is only by doing this that it can protect its core from immediately disintegrating.

I live through an alliance between hot and cold. I would die of passion alone, burst into bits, be split into impotent manifold ardour, able to do nothing. I would not be moved by sympathy, not even for myself. And I would grow quite numb with only the cold, remain in clever indifference, even with regard to my own existence, my own fate. I can only go out into the world in the alliance between hot and cold, endure living on and finding the force and courage to act: strength through heat, and courage through coldness. (140)

What is said here about hot and cold touches the central aspect of Gyllensten's dialectical tension: surrender and distance are forces which work against each other, but by doing so they also form an alliance with each other. Gyllensten often describes this play of forces in Existential and even biological terms, and one could say that it penetrates man's basic Existential condition. In the end the tension between surrender and distance goes together with the rhythm from spiritual death and destruction to new life and creation, which may be found in so many of Gyllensten's novels.

III   *The Author in his Times*

The formula of surrender and distance is also useful in placing Gyllensten's writing in his times. His work began with two books which directly placed surrender and distance against each other as two dialectically opposed alternatives. *Modern Myths* develops the possibility of meeting an absurd world with an attitude which means "living without spontaneity, naïveté, involvement, or faith, but with an always active, illusionless will instead" (171). In the prayer to ordinary, everyday life which concludes the book it becomes completely clear that this attitude rejects all pathetic gestures and adventurous enterprises. In *The Blue Ship*, however, Gyllensten presented another attitude which means "irrevocably surrendering oneself to what is offered, with the complete knowledge that it will perhaps not succeed but kill" (180). This possibility is presented as a miracle: in the last chapter the mother, Emma, walks over the water and thus demonstrates the way of surrender.

One could say that these two books, with dialectically sharp clarity, pointed out the two poles between which the subsequent works would move. In one way, the line to *Infantilia* is clear: the protagonist of the novel, Karl-Erik, is torn between the two attitudes described in the previous books. But in *Infantilia* the tension between the two possibilities appears painful and devastating. Helplessly split, Karl-Erik cannot feel at home with any of the alternatives, is instead broken down and destroyed. At the same time surrender received another tone. As opposed to the light and affirmative surrender in *The Blue Ship*, *Infantilia* describes a somber and destructive surrender which finally leads to murder and suicide.

If Gyllensten's first two books juxtaposed the possibilities of surrender and distance, the novels of the second period were all written under the sign of distance. In contrast to the dangerous surrender in *Infantilia*, *Senilia* develops a distanced attitude whose aim is to recognize and disarm destructive impulses and attitudes. One might say that Karl-Erik in *Infantilia* incarnates the somber surrender in Gyllensten's authorship more completely than any other of his characters: he is a desperado. In *Senilia* Karl-Erik returns as Gunnar Gren, but is exposed to a stubborn and thorough-going criticism by the protagonist of the novel. This Torsten Lerr is in turn the foremost representative of the reasonable distance in Gyllensten's work and it is also Thorsten Lerr's line which is followed up in *The Senator* and *The Death of Socrates*. In both of these novels the narrator adopts a reserved and critical position in relation to his characters and, as in *Senilia*, different forms of somber surrender are illuminated and discarded. Both Senator Bhör and Socrates are, each in his own way, strongly attracted to death and disintegration. In many ways they have good ground for their actions, but they nevertheless get lost and more or less actively seek their own deaths. Thus they become desperadoes like Karl-Erik, and using Erik Hjalmar Linder's words, one could say that the novels during the second period formulate a criticism of different "dangerous convictions."[4] Perhaps one can best summarize the attitude of distance as a radical humanism: the simple everyday life is protected against convictions and enterprises which are bad for us. It is important to underline that this is a position characteristic of the 1940's. Gyllensten's reserved attitude ought, it seems, to be seen as a personally designed variation of the profound skepticism of the 1940's of all seductive ideologies and dogmas of salvation.

However, Gyllensten abandoned this position during the third period, and the novels which followed may be seen as an expression of a renewed light surrender. Toward the middle of the 1960's a change in the intellectual climate in Sweden took place which was just as radical as the change brought about by the experiences of World War II in the 1940's. The war in Vietnam paved the way for strong international involvement and violent criticism of different forms of imperialism. At the same time eyes were turned toward Swedish society, and the welfare state was suddenly shown to have great flaws. The socialistic ideas received a strong renaissance, structuralistic ideas were introduced from France especially, and ecological points of view were given great weight. This powerful and broad series of events was of the type that touched practically everyone and there is no doubt that Gyllensten was strongly influenced by it. During the first half of the 1960's, the strongly anti-ideological attitude of the 1940's appeared to be less fruitful for him—even though he maintained much of his critical attitude in the future as well. It was this decampment which was given form in *Cain's Memoirs* and *Juvenilia*, and in both novels iconoclasm therefore played a central role: the strategy is to blow up outmoded patterns and images in order to see and experience in a new way. It was no longer a question of rejecting different dangerous convictions, but of seeking out new ideas and possibilities for action. What primarily characterizes these books is a basic attitude of searching, and in his subsequent novels Gyllensten worked toward what one could call a structuralistic way of looking at things. He paid more and more attention to the forces and patterns which steer our lives and emphasized the interplay between human beings and their surroundings and the way people belong together. The key word for this new attitude is *participation*.

With the whole of Gyllensten's authorship to date in perspective, therefore, one may speak of a development from a clearly individualistic position to a view of human beings incorporated in a meaningful interplay with their surroundings and fellow human beings.[5] In *Modern Myths*, especially, but also in the ironically narrated novels, there is a defiant repudiation of atrocious reality which has an almost anarchistic tone. This position has to do not only with the experience of standing on the sidelines, but is also a question of desiring to stand on the outside. Perhaps one could even say that in Gyllensten's earliest epistemological statements there is a tendency to place such great weight on the significance of the subject in the process of knowledge that reality fades away. The short story "The Tower of Women" in *Modern Myths* is a very clear expression of this extreme individualism. It is not only the fact that the man who tries out six different styles of life on the six working days of the week is completely free and independent to go between the most varied forms of life, but on the seventh day he relaxes on the beach like the Creator himself above all of his styles of life.

A scene from *In the Shadow of Don Juan* can be placed in contrast to "The Tower of Women." It occurs in the beginning of the novel and describes the end of Juanito's love affair with the older woman. One morning when everything is over he sneaks away to see her one last time. She lives in two small rooms above the stable, and he finds her, her husband, and their children sleeping close together. He remains sitting there and everything moves very close to him. He sinks down into a sea of noises, smells, and feelings; and inside him grows a great, happy melancholy:

The sea, the sea of the living surrounded him: he swam in it and drowned in it at the same time; he was born by it and carried by it and swallowed or soaked by it. He felt more closely than ever before, and perhaps more than ever after, how everything and everyone fit together in one huge, limitless unity of life and likeness, in the same fate and the same conditions—in desire and zeal, in toil, despair, happiness, death. (56)

In a broad historical perspective one could characterize Gyllensten's continuous coming to terms with the masters in his novels from the third period as a criticism of Western individualism which connotes arrogant conceit and ruthless power practices and exploitation. All of the temptation of this ideal is in his novels, but it is just therefore that they convincingly demonstrate that that road leads out into the empty desert. Instead a kind of humility is born: a recognition of the forces which steer our lives, which does not stand in opposition to the resolute will to do that which is in our power. With this humility also follows the feeling of being at home in existence.

This new attitude is not, however, an intellectual insight alone, but also the result of a profound emotional process. In many of Gyllensten's earlier novels the suffering of the world stands in sharp contrast to the powerlessness of the individual human being. But in his latest novels there is a much more harmonious view of man's position in the world. Perhaps one could say that the individual human being receives a responsibility which more realistically corresponds to his capacity, and thus the crippling feeling of guilt for the situation in the world gives way and is replaced by peace. The experience of the exposed situation of man in the world is no less intense, but it is balanced by a newborn power to act—which is not to say that this new attitude is without complications nor that Gyllensten's authorship has come to a definite endpoint. But one may see the development in his authorship as a part of a great intellectual and emotional process of reorientation which has been clearly expressed both in political thought and in art during the past ten years. For his readers, therefore, his novels offer an opportunity to test their own experiences and points of view at a profound level. For himself, Gyllensten's writing is an intensive attempt at finding a tenable attitude toward life, and his readers can therefore in turn make use of his authorship to orient themselves in our increasingly threatened world.

Notes and References

Chapter One

1. This biographical section is based on an extensive written reply to an interview which Gyllensten submitted for this book in December 1974. In my presentation of Gyllensten's goals for his writing, my point of departure has been the many program articles which he has written over the years. The greater part of these articles is printed in the two essay collections entitled *Nihilistiskt credo (Nihilistic Credo)* (1964) and *Ur min offentliga sektor (From My Public Sector)* (1971) from which I have quoted.

2. Gyllensten's uncertainty in his choice of profession and his negative experience of his medical studies recur in Torsten Mannelin's diary entries from his period as a young medical student in the novel *Juvenilia* from 1965 (49–51 and 57–59). However, as in the other novels, Gyllensten only used the biographical material as a point of departure and treated it freely for the purposes of the novel.

3. Gyllensten's research mainly falls into four different fields. In his doctoral dissertation he dealt with the growth of the thymus and the lymphatic system. During the 1950's he succeeded in demonstrating experimentally that a serious eye disease occurring in newborn babies was the result of oxygen poisoning. After that he primarily devoted himself to the investigation of the significance of visual impressions for the development of the higher sight centers and measurements of the white blood cells which the thymus releases into the blood. All in all he has published well over forty scientific articles.

4. *Nihilistic Credo*, pp. 47–48.

5. *Ibid.*, p. 20.

6. *From My Public Sector*, pp. 81–83.

7. Erik Hjalmar Linder, *Fem decennier av nittonhundratalet* (Stockholm: Natur och kultur, 1965–66), p. 994.

8. Reprinted in *From My Public Sector*, pp. 83–89.

9. *Dagens Nyheter*, December 30, 1972.

10. *Nihilistic Credo*, pp. 52–53.

11. *From My Public Sector*, p. 181.

12. *Ibid.*, p. 96.

13. *Ibid.*, p. 81.
14. *Ibid.*, p. 80.
15. Hans-Erik Johannesson, *Studier i Lars Gyllenstens estetik* (Göteborg: Göteborgs universitet, 1973), pp. 4–6.
16. *From My Public Sector*, p. 150.
17. Artur Lundkvist (editor), *Författare tar ståndpunkt* (Stockholm: Tiden, 1960), pp. 71–72.
18. *Vänkritik. 22 samtal om dikt tillägnade Olle Holmberg* (Stockholm: Bonniers, 1959), p. 42.
19. *Svensk litteraturtidskrift*, January–March 1953, p. 18.
20. *Aftonbladet*, September 16, 1970.
21. Erik Hjalmar Linder, *Fem decennier av nittonhundratalet* (Stockholm: Natur och kultur, 1965–66), pp. 787 and 793.
22. Karl Vennberg and Werner Aspenström (editors), *Kritiskt 40-tal* (Stockholm: Bonniers, 1948), p. 233.
23. Karl Vennberg, *Dikter 1944–1949* (Stockholm: Bonniers, 1953), p. 10.
24. Gunnar Brandell, *Svensk litteratur 1900–1950* (Stockholm: Bonniers, 1967), pp. 337–339.
25. Karl Vennberg and Werner Aspenström (editors), *Kritiskt 40-tal* (Stockholm: Bonniers, 1948), p. 241.
26. Erik Hjalmar Linder, *Fem decennier av nittonhundratalet* (Stockholm: Natur och kultur, 1965–66), p. 794.
27. *Dagens Nyheter*, June 9, 1972.
28. *Utsikt*, March 1950, p. 3.
29. *Nihilistic Credo*, p. 20.
30. *Utsikt*, March 1950, p. 4.
31. *BMF*, May 1956, p. 7.
32. Artur Lundkvist (editor), *Författare tar ståndpunkt* (Stockholm: Tiden, 1960), p. 70.
33. *Nihilistic Credo*, p. 19.
34. *Ibid.*, p. 31.
35. Hans-Erik Johannesson, *Studier i Lars Gyllenstens estetik* (Göteborg: Göteborgs universitet, 1973), pp. 10–21.
36. *Dagens Nyheter*, June 9, 1972.
37. *Nihilistic Credo*, pp. 9–13.
38. *Ibid.*, p. 33.
39. *Ibid.*
40. *From My Public Sector*, pp. 139–42.
41. *Vänkritik. 22 samtal om dikt tillägnade Olle Holmberg* (Stockholm: Bonniers, 1959), pp. 41–42.
42. *Utsikt*, March 1949, p. 14.

43. *Vintergatan 1960*, p. 60.
44. *Nihilistic Credo*, p. 86.
45. *Ibid.*, p. 42.
46. *Ibid.*, p. 26.
47. *From My Public Sector*, p. 185.
48. *Ibid.*, p. 175.

Chapter Two

1. It is, however, hardly a question of a direct influence from Camus. There is probably a literary connection through Kierkegaard: perhaps the furiously disciplined Assessor Wilhelm in *Either - Or* lies behind Gyllensten's hero, and Camus also built upon Kierkegaard. But what is important here is the fact that a heroic resistance seemed to be the only adequate reaction to the situation during and after World War II for both Camus and Gyllensten.

2. An article on Martin Buber provides a representative expression of Gyllensten's attitude. In it Gyllensten claims that religious authors like Buber, Dante, and Kierkegaard also permit secular readings. The fact that the religious systems present metaphysical ideas which are no longer tenable today does not mean that the religious languages are uninteresting or unusable. He formulates his own experience of their fruitfulness in the following way: "The religious languages are collective creations, nourished and enriched by the experiences and imagination of generations, and they serve as aids for human beings in interpreting reality, describing it, understanding it, relating to it, and establishing contact with it in general" *(From My Public Sector*, p. 128).

3. *Svensk litteraturtidskrift*, January–March 1953, p. 19.
4. *Bonniers litterära magasin* XXXII (April 1963), p. 287.
5. *Ibid.*, p. 288.
6. More specifically it is Ingemar Hedenius's philosophical book *Tro och vetande* (Stockholm: Bonniers, 1949), which Gyllensten aims at in *Carnivora* (68–71).

Chapter Three

1. *Bonniers litterära magasin* XXIV (August 1955), p. 620.
2. *Ibid.*, p. 619.
3. In *Senilia* very exact points in time are given for the events which Torsten remembers. The present moment of the novel is an autumn day in 1955. The dates of some of the most important events of the past can perhaps give an idea of the complicated family story comprised by Torsten's memories:

1860 — Torsten's father is born.
1917 — Torsten is born.
1927 — His father is blind.
1932 — His father dies, Ester is born.
1936 — Torsten graduates from high school.
1941 — Major Klingsor dies.
1948 — Gunnar and Elsa marry.
1951 — Gunnar almost murders Ester's child.
1953 — Gunhild and Elsa die.

4. Gyllensten has directly referred to Proust's great series of novels *À la recherche du temps perdu* in the chapter devoted to Torsten's father: À la recherche du père perdu.

5. Örjan Lindberger, "Att avväpna smärtan," *Bonniers litterära magasin* XXVI (June 1957), p. 497.

6. *Ibid.*

7. *Bonniers litterära magasin* XXIV (August 1955), p. 618 cont.

8. *Return to Ithaca* is subtitled "A Novel About the Present."

9. *Vintergatan 1960*, p. 56. Gyllensten wrote the diary at the invitation of this annual literary magazine.

10. Sven-Eric Liedman, "Mänskligt och omänskligt. Om Lars Gyllenstens författarskap," *Svensk litteraturtidskrift*, January 1966, p. 31 cont.

11. In the short stories there are also different personal constellations than the ones in *Senilia*. In "Slap Across the Face," for example, the connection with the novel is obvious. But the novel's Gunnar appears to be divided into two people: Gunnar and Greger.

Chapter Four

1. *Bonniers litterära magasin* XXXIII (August 1964), p. 579.

2. *Bonniers litterära magasin* XXXI (May 1962), p. 348.

3. *Bonniers litterära magasin* XXXIII (August 1964), p. 579.

4. *Ibid.*

5. There is another direct reference back to *Cain's Memoirs* in the motto of *Juvenilia*, which consists of quotations from the two brief fragments about Cain. The two first sentences of the motto are found in the second fragment and in its final sentence in the first fragment (144, Eng. tr. 97, and 109, Eng. tr. 73, respectively).

6. In an interview Gyllensten has even spoken about *Cain's Memoirs* as Mannelin's work of art (*Vår lösen*, September 1965)!

7. *Bonniers litterära magasin* XXXIII (August 1964), p. 579.

8. Gyllensten quotes the Swedish translation and it is even more seductive: "Allt är skönt på vår fjärran kust, / allt är blott lyx och

lugn och lust." (In prose translation: "On our foreign coast pleasure reigns, / life is only luxury and peace and desire.")
  9. 57 cont., 102 cont., 121 cont., and 130 cont.

Chapter Five

1. The collage aspect was also emphasized by the fact that the covers of *The Palace in the Park* and *The Cave in the Desert* are picture collages whose different elements refer to the people and milieus of the novels.
2. *From My Public Sector*, p. 163 cont.
3. *Ibid.*, p. 165. (The interview was first published in the newsletter of a book club: *Kikaren*, November 1970. However, the section quoted in which Gyllensten proclaims the effect of myths throughout history most emphatically was written in connection with the reprinting of the article in *From My Public Sector*.
4. Maud Bodkin, *Archetypal Patterns in Poetry* (London: Oxford University Press, 1968), p. 54.
5. *From My Public Sector*, p. 179.
6. See also pp. 59 cont., 67, 138, and 183.
7. In the back cover text written by Gyllensten himself he declared that he had gone back to Tirso de Molina's story about "a self-satisfied, arrogant Don Juan who defied God and men and all common sense and propriety." This view of Don Juan precedes the interpretation of Don Juan as a libertine.

Chapter Six

1. Wayne C. Booth, *The Rhetoric of Fiction* (Chicago: The University of Chicago Press, 1966), p. 23.
2. *Nihilistic Credo*, p. 31.
3. Kerstin Munck, *Gyllenstens roller. En studie över tematik och gestaltning i Lars Gyllenstens författarskap* (Lund, 1974), p. 13.
4. Erik Hjalmar Linder, *Fem decennier av nittonhundratalet* (Stockholm: Natur och kultur, 1965–66), p. 1002.
5. This interpretation gets further support in a collection of excerpts from his note books which Gyllensten published in the fall of 1976—*Lapptäcken - Livstecken* (*Patchwork Quilts - Tokens of Life*).

Selected Bibliography

PRIMARY SOURCES

1. Lars Gyllensten: works of fiction

Camera obscura. (Together with Torgny Greitz.) Stockholm: Bonniers, 1946.
Moderna myter (Modern Myths). Stockholm: Bonniers, 1949.
Det blå skeppet (The Blue Ship). Stockholm: Bonniers, 1950.
Barnabok (Infantilia). Stockholm: Bonniers, 1952.
Carnivora. Stockholm: Bonniers, 1953.
Senilia. Stockholm: Bonniers, 1956.
Senatorn (The Senator). Stockholm: Bonniers, 1958.
Sokrates död (The Death of Socrates). Stockholm: Bonniers, 1960.
Desperados (Desperadoes). Stockholm: Bonniers, 1962.
Kains memoarer (Cain's Memoirs). Stockholm: Bonniers, 1963.
Juvenilia. Stockholm: Bonniers, 1965.
Lotus i Hades (Lotus in Hades). Stockholm: Bonniers, 1966.
Diarium spirituale. Stockholm: Bonniers, 1968.
Palatset i parken (The Palace in the Park). Stockholm: Bonniers, 1970.
Människan djuren all naturen (Man, Animals, All of Nature). Stockholm: Bonniers, 1971.
Grottan i öknen (The Cave in the Desert). Stockholm: Bonniers, 1973.
I skuggan av Don Juan (In the Shadow of Don Juan). Stockholm: Bonniers, 1975.
Lapptäcken-Livstecken. Stockholm: Författarförlaget, 1976.

2. Lars Gyllensten: collections of articles and essays

Nihilistiskt credo (Nihilistic Credo). Stockholm: Bonniers, 1964.
Ur min offentliga sektor (From My Public Sector). Stockholm: Aldus/Bonniers, 1971.

3. Lars Gyllensten: articles and essays not reprinted in *Nihilistic Credo* or *From My Public Sector*

"Arrogant snusförnuft om barock och klassicism." *Utsikt,* February 1949, pp. 2–4.

"Femtio bokläsare redovisar sina största litterära upplevelser." *Horisont* (Vasa), January-February, 1958, p. 8.
"40-tal och 70-tal — likt och olikt." *Dagens Nyheter*, August 3, 1972.
Författare tar ståndpunkt. Stockholm: Tiden, 1960, pp. 69–75.
"Kortsvar till Karl Vennberg." *Aftonbladet*, September 9, 1970.
"Lars Gyllensten: Barnabok." *Svensk litteraturtidskrift*, January–March 1953, pp. 18–20.
"Min klassiker: Sören Kierkegaard." *Utsikt*, March 1949, pp. 14–15.
"Nazistolympiaden går igen." *Dagens Nyheter*, December 30, 1972.
Note to a chapter from *Cain's Memoirs* entitled "Kainitiska fragment." *Bonniers litterära magasin* XXXI (May 1962), p. 348.
Note to a chapter from *Juvenilia* entitled "Inkarnationer." *Bonniers litterära magasin* XXXIII (August 1964), p. 579.
"Om att skriva böcker." *BMF*, May 1956, pp. 6–7.
"Ord: notiser till ett författarskap." *Utsikt*, March 1950, pp. 2–5.
"Reflexer." *Vintergatan*, 1960, pp. 51–61.
"Senatorns ändalykt." *Vänkritik. 22 samtal om dikt tillägnade Olle Holmberg.* Stockholm: Bonniers, 1959, pp. 38–43.
"Senilia. Tankar kring berättande och kring Thomas Mann." *Bonniers litterära magasin* XXIV (August 1955), pp. 618–22.
"Så skrev vi då en kväll diktsamlingen Camera obscura." *Dagens Nyheter*, June 9, 1972.
"Ur arbetsböckerna. En baklängestur." *Bonniers litterära magasin* XXXVI (June 1967), pp. 408–16.

SECONDARY SOURCES

BJÖRCK, STAFFAN. *Romanens formvärld.* Stockholm: Natur och Kultur, 1953.
BODKIN, MAUD. *Archetypal Patterns in Poetry.* London: Oxford paperbacks, 1968 (First edition 1934).
BOOTH, WAYNE C. *The Rhetoric of Fiction.* Chicago: The University of Chicago Press, 1966 (First edition 1961).
ISAKSSON, HANS. "Lars Gyllenstens 'Juvenilia.'" *Den moderne roman og romanforskning i Norden.* Bergen, Oslo, Tromsø: Universitetsforlaget, 1971, pp. 16–30.
————. *Hängivenhet och distans. En studie i Lars Gyllenstens romankonst.* Dissertation with a summary in English. Stockholm: Aldus/Bonniers, 1974.
IVARSSON, NILS IVAR. "Senatorns ändalykt." *Vänkritik. 22 samtal om dikt tillägnade Olle Holmberg.* Stockholm: Bonniers, 1959, pp. 31–38.

Selected Bibliography

JOHANNESSON, HANS-ERIK. *Studier i Lars Gyllenstens estetik. Hans teorier om författarskapets villkor och teknik t.o.m. Barnabok.* Dissertation with a summary in German. Göteborg: Litteraturvetenskapliga institutionen vid Göteborgs universitet, 1973.

LAGERLÖF, KARL ERIK. "Utbrytningsförsök." *Samtal med 00-talister.* Stockholm: Bonniers, 1965, pp. 27–38.

LEVIN, HARRY. *James Joyce. A Critical Introduction.* London: Faber paper covered editions, 1971 (First edition 1944).

LIEDMAN, SVEN-ERIC. "Mänskligt och omänskligt. Operationalism och existentialism i Lars Gyllenstens författarskap." *Svensk litteraturtidskrift,* January–March 1966, pp. 24–39.

LINDBERGER, ÖRJAN. "Att avväpna smärtan." *Bonniers litterära magasin* XXVI (June 1957), pp. 496–501.

LINDER, ERIK HJ. *Fem decennier av nittonhundratalet.* Stockholm: Natur och Kultur, 1965–66, pp. 994–1004.

MUNCK, KERSTIN. *Gyllenstens roller. En studie över tematik och gestaltning i Lars Gyllenstens författarskap.* Dissertation with a summary in English. Lund: CWK Gleerup, 1974.

PALMQVIST, BERTIL. "Satsa på undret. Lars Gyllenstens dialektiska trilogi." *Bonniers litterära magasin,* XXXII (April 1963), pp. 282–88.

SJÖBERG, LEIF. "Lars Gyllensten: Masters of arts and science." *The American-Scandinavian Review,* February 1967, pp. 158–62.

STENSTRÖM, THURE. "Lars Gyllenstens Senilia — en roman om tiden." *Berättartekniska studier.* Stockholm: Svenska Bokförlaget/Bonniers, 1964, pp. 21–39.

STOLPE, JAN. "Förtrogenhetens färla och djurfällens instängda värme." *Femtiotalet i backspegeln.* Stockholm: Aldus/Bonniers, 1968, pp. 35–47.

VENNBERG, KARL. "Den moderna pessimismen och dess vedersakare." *Kritiskt 40-tal.* Stockholm: Bonniers, 1948, pp. 226–41.

TRANSLATIONS OF LARS GYLLENSTEN'S WORKS

1. English

The Testament of Cain. London: Calder and Boyars, 1967.

2. French

Infantilia. Paris: Gallimard, 1969.

3. German

Desperados (eight of the fourteen stories in the Swedish edition).
   Stuttgart: Deutsche Verlags-Anstalt, 1965.
Kains Memoiren. Frankfurt: Suhrkamp, 1968.

Index

(The works of Gyllensten are listed under his name)